Break The Mold

pursuing a life of servanthood

BRIAN ROSE
WITH ALICIA ROSE

Break The Mold – pursuing a life of servanthood

Unless otherwise indicated, Bible quotations are taken from the New International Version. Copyright 1973, 1978, 1984 by Zondervan Publishing House.

Scripture quotations marked MSG are from the The Message by Eugene H. Peterson. Copyright 1993, 1994, 1995, 1996, 2000.

Scripture quotations marked NKJV are from THE NEW KING JAMES VERSION. Copyright 1982.

Cover design by BespokeBookCovers.com

ISBN 10: 1722642351
ISBN 13: 978-1722642358

CONTENTS

acknowledgments

This book is dedicated to greatest servant-leader who ever lived—Jesus. Every day I try to learn new ways to reflect His heart to serve Him and our world better.

Also to my favorite person on the planet, Alicia, who is second-best thing that's ever happened to me. There's no one in the world I'd rather share life with.

And to my best friends, Kaitlyn, Makayla, Riley, Brooklyn, London, and Jude—I love you more than life.

To the people of VIVE Culture, thank you for staying up late, waking up early, and showing up week-in-and-week-out to serve our city and beyond. It's one of the greatest honors of my life to serve our House. This book shares our journey in what we want to see happen in our city.

I especially wanted to thank everyone who shared in this book journey with me:

Tori Cawman and Cory Stuefer, thank you for taking time to help with the first edits for this book. I really appreciate you.

To our brilliant, professional editor, Karen Engle—you brought the whole thing to life. It was a joy to work with you.

To Peter O'Connor who designed our book cover, thank you for patiently working through the process with us.

Thank you Jill Stuefer who helped shape the title of this book.

To our VIVE leadership team: thank you for showing up every single week ready to pour your lives into creating space for people to flourish in the call they have on their lives. There is not a team on the planet I'd rather do life with than you guys.

Some of the best memories I have growing up were our Rose Family Road Trips.

Every year my dad would take his red pen and map out every state we would visit on his road atlas. Those are what they used back in the dinosaur days before we had GPS systems and Siri to take us around the world. My dad would strategically plan every detail. He was walking that fine line between genius and insanity. Only a chief master sergeant who served in the military could be so detailed to plan every bathroom stop.

Who can plan when you have to use the restroom? Apparently, my dad could. That's right, I was raised old school. He figured out the amount of gas it would take down to the gallon, marked every rest stop, and had every kind of safety tool you would ever need just in case the apocalypse happened.

I always looked forward to our road trips growing up. We would load up our medium-size White Chevy, popped fresh batteries in our Walkman radios, made sure we had our mixed cassette tapes full of songs we ripped from the radio, and headed out on the open road.

When I was growing up we didn't have Blu-ray players, iPhones, or iPads to keep us entertained. In those days, my two brothers and I had to find creative ways to entertain ourselves. One way we did that was by taking my mom's boom box that could record our voices and pretend we were sports analysts on ESPN. We would do that for hours at a time.

One year my parents surprised us by taking us to the Grand Canyon. Of course, I had heard about this historic destination in school and saw pictures of it in textbooks. However, nothing could prepare me for what I was about to behold.

I'll never forget seeing the Grand Canyon for the first time. The vastness of the mountains and the depth of the canyons struck a little fear in me. The mountains seemed like they went on forever. It was truly remarkable. I never saw such beauty in all of my life. When I was five years old, we moved away from all of my family in Chicago, Illinois, and landed in Southern California because my mom's health couldn't take the cold weather any longer. So, most of my life, we were surrounded by mountains every single day. But it was nothing like what I was I taking in.

This opened my eyes to something I knew existed but never experienced firsthand. There's a vast difference between reading about something in a history book and personally experiencing something.

It was the first time in my life I remember being full of awe and wonder.

As we were taking in the sites, I remember there was this married couple next to us that wouldn't stop fighting with one another. It was clear that they had a lot of issues they were trying to work out. However, as a kid, I just thought they were being annoying. So I did what any ten-year-old kid would do. I just stared at them with a dirty look and hoped that would give them a hint to go away.

Apparently my child-like glare didn't strike fear in them quite like I hoped.

The arguments persisted and they began to take their frustrations out on their kids. At first I was annoyed, but that shifted as I started feeling sorry for their kids. Their faces were full of sadness. They were staring out at the majestic scenery, but they weren't captivated like the rest of us. They seemed to be numb to it all. They certainly weren't struck with awe and wonder.

Everyone around us was taking pictures, enjoying the moment, and soaking it all in. This family had arrived at the destination they set out for and missed the whole point.

How can someone look at what I was seeing and not be stirred to want to know more about this Creator who is behind it all? How can two people be looking at the same thing and have two completely different experiences? How could they be looking at something so magnificent and miss it entirely?

Life can be a lot like that. We can pour our time, money, and energy into getting to a certain place in life, and once we arrive, miss the whole point of why we are there in the first place.

Some people spend their entire lives pursuing a certain way of living only to find out in the end that it was all for nothing.

A FRESH VANTAGE POINT

As I continue to embark on this incredible journey called life, there are certain phrases, mindsets, and world views that many people have adopted that seem to have taken away from the mission of what we are called to be like in this world . . . a people group set apart to serve our city and world with the love and grace that we've been shown through Christ.

There's no question about it. These are exciting days that we are living in as leaders. There has never been more information at our disposal on what it takes to be a successful leader than right now. We have more leadership conferences than ever before, and we can listen to the best leadership minds with a click of a button, absolutely free.

Ten years ago, you would have to spend thousands of dollars for your team to fly to another state, get a hotel, and attend a leadership conference to hear the top teachings on leadership. Now you can stream it for free while you run on the treadmill. If you walk into any bookstore, there are thousands of books lined up on the topic of leadership.

Everyone is on a never-ending search to answer this one question: How do I become a somebody?

Let me be clear up front. I'm a sucker for leadership books. One of my favorite leadership minds has to be Craig Groeschel, lead pastor of Life.Church. I'm a sponge every time he releases a leadership podcast.

This book is in no way an anti-leadership book. Rather, this book is designed to encourage others to think about pursuing a life of servanthood. Spirits that learn how to follow and serve faithfully produce the best leaders.

What if we asked ourselves every single day, "How can I learn to serve others better?" How can I leverage what I have and what I know to make someone else better?"

Pursuing a life of servanthood isn't something to muddle through. It's something we are called to for a lifetime. We never graduate from pursuing a life of servanthood.

What if we pursued a life of servanthood as much as we pursued a mind for leadership? Think of how different our world would be if our homes, workplaces, schools, and churches were full of servant-leaders.

[When you look at leadership through the lens of Scripture, it's not about being in charge. Leadership is about caring for those people in our charge.] It's a whole new way of looking at leadership.

To break the mold literally means to put an end to a restrictive pattern of events or behavior by doing things in a markedly different way.

[I believe that if we can break the mold on this idea of servanthood and embrace the spirit of a servant-leader, God will open up doors that would never be possible any other way.]

I'm not going to lie to you; there are going to be parts in this book that will be uncomfortable and hard to read, and will challenge your way of living. And I don't have all the answers. I'm on the same journey as each of you trying to learn what a life of servanthood really looks like through the eyes of Christ.

But I hope that the real life stories I share as a parent, mixed with the funny moments I've failed as a dad, combined with lessons in the Bible end up compelling you to pursue a new way of living.

Even if you aren't a follower of Jesus, I believe there are life lessons in here that you can pull from that can better your life.

I pray as you move through these pages you will feel the grace of God over your life, and your spirit will be encouraged to see the season of life you are in just a little differently. Every season of your life has meaning and purpose. You can still be a great leader even if you aren't in charge. You can still make a lasting impact even if no one knows your name. You still can be a blessing to people around you everywhere you find yourself.

Nothing is ever wasted in the hands of Jesus.

ONE FINAL NOTE

My intention for this book is that you break the mold in certain areas of your life and realize that pursuing a life of servanthood actually frees your soul to be able to flourish wherever you are planted. This way of living releases you to serve your city, family, leaders, and circle of influence in an even greater way.

There are many books out there that are written perfectly with some of the best publishers and writers who make everything flow seamlessly. I admire those authors. This isn't one of those books. That's just not me.

There are also books written by ghostwriters, but it's not my personality to have another person write for me. I write with my heart. Some chapters may be shorter than others. It will be a bit messy, raw, and very personal.

I write with complete vulnerability. For some people, that may be new for you. For others, it may be surprisingly refreshing. I write the way I would talk in person. This book was written in the backyard with my kids playing hoops, in a coffee shop in the city, on the couch surrounded by piles of laundry, in bed late at night with my wife fast asleep next to me, and sitting in the streetcar cruising in downtown Kansas City.

This book is merely a collection of my experiences, failures, and life lessons that have led me to this point in my life.

It's my heart. My passion. My voice.

And I hope by the end of it you feel encouraged to serve your sphere of influence even better!

So, whether you are on a serious pursuit of knowing Jesus, a casual spectator, or simply curious, I pray that your heart would be lifted to know God and with that revelation you would be stirred to lift others up around you.

I pray we commit in a greater way to live a life of servanthood.

The goal through it all is for you to experience Jesus, and for Him to be pushed to the front and center of it all. Because when a person pursues Jesus, it changes everything.

I'm convinced that when people have a true collision with the Living God, there is this glorious havoc that happens inside of the very core of their being that wrecks everything . . . in the best kind of way!

1

ride or die

Back when I was twenty-eight-years old, life seemed much simpler. My wife, Alicia, and I have been married for thirteen years and have six amazing kids. However, back then we had only been married for a couple years and we were about to have our second child. I never knew I could love someone so much just by touching their little fingers.

Being a husband and father is a dream. I know we don't hear that much anymore, but it's true.

But as much as I loved being a husband and being a father, something seemed to be missing in me. When we were first married we had this clear vision that we would one day pastor our own church. This seemed impossible because we were newly married, had no kids, and were living in a 550-square-foot apartment in San Diego with no real experience under our belts.

We didn't know where or how it would happen, but we just knew God placed this calling on our lives to lead a relational, refreshing, relevant church in a city. We were so excited! Probably like most young couples with no kids, we thought we were going to get a call the next week for our dream job.

That wasn't the case for us. We served at a great church in San Diego before we were hired to be the family pastors at another large church in

Southern California. We loved serving the vision of our former pastors. In fact, my former pastors in California are still mentors to me, and good friends of mine even to this day. Back then when we became the family pastors in Southern California, we just had our second baby girl and we were pastoring a thriving ministry. I loved serving under that leadership! But something in me still was waiting for that promise to lead our own church.

The unexpected day came when our pastor told us that a change was coming for him and his family and he would be taking a new role pastoring pastors. I was happy for him, but my heart was also sad because I loved serving alongside him.

The church began the search for a new lead pastor and through that process I knew without a doubt that the church I was serving at wasn't a right fit for my family and me.

The frustration continued to build inside of my young heart. One stormy night I snuck out of the house when everyone was asleep and locked myself in my church's auditorium to pray. I sat at the piano and began to play. I would love to say what came out of my mouth was nothing but gratitude.

However, it was actually the opposite. So much frustration had built up in my heart that I couldn't take it anymore—and I let it all out on that stage. It had been a few years since we heard anything from God about this call we felt when we were first married. What changed?

It seemed like the doors of heaven shut on us everywhere we turned. There were no opportunities. There were no words from God. There were no promotions.

Just silence.

Did we make it up? Was it bad pizza from the night before? How could we receive such a clear vision from God and have no outlet to walk it out?

I felt stuck. Abandoned. And to make it worse, I felt guilty for feeling that way. I felt as if God was disappointed with me for feeling the way I did.

How ungrateful could I be, right?

I was serving at a large church, married to the woman of my dreams, and blessed with two incredible kids. What more could I ask for?

However, when I looked around, it seemed like everyone was living my dream. Have you ever had that feeling? Like everyone else is moving forward in life and you are stuck? My friends were the ones planting churches. Staff members I served with were leaving to be part of even bigger churches. Colleagues I served with were now speaking at leadership conferences. My pastor was about to transition out. Everyone was moving into their dream home. And me . . . well, I *just* served.

There was nothing glamorous about it. I felt like I was missing out on life. As I was sitting at the piano, I felt Jesus speak to my heart.

I felt Jesus ask, "Do you trust Me?"

Being a pastor I had to answer yes, right? If I didn't, what kind of Christian would I be? But I'm going to be honest, I didn't say yes right away. I paused. Did I really trust Him? Or was I more in love with the idea of the promise?

"If I'm being honest, I'm not exactly sure what you see in me," I told Him.

That was the truth. What it really came down to wasn't that I felt abandoned. I just didn't think I was worthy or capable of leading well.

Of course, Jesus didn't let the question go. He asked again, "Do you trust Me?"

"I'm trying," I said.

I'll never forget what He said to me that night. To paraphrase it, He reminded me of the promise, but told me I wasn't ready to lead yet. My idea of leading was totally different than what Jesus had in mind for His Church.

Jesus spoke to my heart and said, "From this point on I want you to be all in. I want you to take risks. I want you lead from your heart and not your head. It won't be perfect but you need to learn to serve someone else's vision as much as you want someone to serve yours. You don't need to learn how to lead . . . you need to learn how to serve."

I'm not a man who cries easy. But that night I cried at the piano and told God that from that day forward I was all in. Even if I never led another thing in my lifetime, I wanted to learn about this way of living that I was missing out on.

I wanted to break the mold in my own life, but had become so obsessed with trying to be the best leader that I missed the whole point of why I was entrusted with leadership in the first place. That's when I committed to walk the unpopular path toward a life of servanthood.

ALL IN

Anything worth doing is worth giving everything you have to. I love that saying, "Ride or die." To me, that means a person is all in and there's no looking back. So many people want to check every box and have every questioned answered before they do anything significant. But anything that will have any lasting impact is worth giving every ounce of who you are to.

When I married my wife I was 110% in love with her. I still am. Even after all these years I come home work and find her in sweats with her hair tied up in a bun and food on her shirt from caring for our six kids all day and my heart is still in love with that lady.

When people get married they go all in and get excited for certain things.

Women go all in for love and for the idea of companionship.

When we get married, men go all in for sex.

Is it okay to be real for a change?

My wife and I are similar in a lot of ways. But there are a few things we are different in. One of those ways is the way we tell stories. My wife loves to tell every single detail, to every single story she hears throughout the day.

Alicia is a superhero mom. Some superheroes wear capes. My superhero wears yoga pants and baggy shirts as she homeschools our six kids, while co-pastoring VIVE Culture with me, taking kids to their events, while still finding time to make homemade meals and make each of us feel so loved. I can't speak enough about how amazing she is.

Since she is around the kids most of the day, when I walk in the door I'm the first adult she's come in contact with all day. So she wants to tell me about every conversation she's had throughout the day.

Now, when I say my wife loves to tell every detail, she has a way of bringing different voices into her stories so you grasp the full picture of how the person explained it. I just want the Cliff Notes version.

Who was upset? Did it get worked out? Does everyone still love each other? Is pasta for dinner?

I know I'm not the only one who is wired like that. I want the highlights. Alicia and I can spend all day together, drive thirty-one hours across the country with our six kids from Kansas City to California, and twenty-eight hours into it she will say, "What are you thinking about right now?"

What am I thinking about after thirty-one hours nonstop in the car with six kids?

This may shock you, but most of the time I'm not thinking of anything when I'm on a road trip.

Let me tell you something about men. There are times in the day where literally nothing is going on inside of our heads. I know it's hard to believe that we can cross forty-three states without one single thought passing through our head. Nevertheless, it's true. *LoL*

The only two thoughts I usually have are sports and "why does our mini-van smell like hot garbage right now?" That's it.

But it's all worth it. When I married Alicia, I was all in. Not one ounce of me looked back. But I was all in with boundaries. I will admit something about myself. I have boundary issues. Apparently in our pre-marriage counseling, this kind of thing was never brought to my attention.

Apparently my wife was raised with the mindset that what's hers is hers and what's mine is hers. If you're married, you know what I'm talking about. I can't tell you how many times I needed the Holy Spirit to restore my soul when I opened the bathroom cabinet and realized that the toothbrush I bought for my mouth was at her sink, wet, and I hadn't used it yet.

The only reason my toothbrush should be wet is if I use it. Obviously my wife feels "all in" means my toothbrush is fair game. I totally, 100% disagree. I had to throw the challenge flag out early on in our marriage and say what a violation of trust that was. Toothbrushes should always be off limits.

My daughters are just as bad. My two older girls, Kaitlyn and Makayla, think that when they run out of their deodorant, my deodorant is free game just because they have the same last name as me. That couldn't be further from the truth. That's nasty.

We all have different ideas of what it means to be all in when it comes to our marriages, our jobs, how we use our gifts, or how we engage in relationships. But one thing we can all agree on, as Christians, is that we are called to a life of servanthood.

Look at this invitation from Jesus that would extend to every generation of what it means to really follow after Him:

> Then Jesus said to His disciples, "If anyone desires to come after me, let him deny himself, and take up his cross, and follow me. For whoever desires to save his life will lose it, and whoever loses his life for my sake will find it."

(Matthew 16:24–25 NHEB)

In this generation, when reading about this extreme and intense invitation Jesus extended to His disciples, the picture most people think of almost instantly is Jesus hanging on a cross for the sins of humanity—but that would not have been the image that would have come to His first-century audience's minds.

When Jesus said this, He hadn't gone to the cross yet. They didn't even know what Jesus would do for them.

Let's listen to Jesus' words again. He didn't say take up *My* cross. He said take up *your* cross. What would have been the image those ancient Jews would have had?

It would have been the image of criminals carrying a cross right before they were nailed to it. It was known as the "death walk."

It was a public spectacle because Rome's leaders wanted everyone to know that if you crossed them, the consequence was death. Jesus had just given a pretty extreme invitation. This wasn't one of those talks where you don't want to offend anyone so they don't leave your church. This was a calling-to-the-carpet moment.

Jesus was saying, "If you want to follow Me and be identified with Me . . . the path you must walk isn't about leadership as much as it is about *follow-ship*."

He was calling them to the death walk of self.

BREAKING THE MOLD IS INCONVENIENT

Let's not pretend that this life I'm suggesting we go all in on is a walk in the park. In fact, it's frustrating at times. It goes against everything we are seeing in modern culture. To learn to follow Jesus, pick up your own cross, and serve others isn't always convenient for peoples' schedules.

In Jesus' day, a Roman officer would at times select an innocent bystander to carry the criminal's cross who was guilty of a certain crime. Talk about being inconvenienced. Who wants to be that guy? Those are the moments you try and avoid eye contact with the teacher so you don't get picked to read in front of the class.

When it was time for Jesus to carry His cross in those final hours, the Roman soldiers picked a man out of the crowd to carry it for Him. I don't know if you know this or not, but Jesus did not carry His own cross the whole way up to his crucifixion. An innocent bystander carried it for Him—a bystander who seemed to be randomly selected. But of course we know God orchestrated the entire interaction.

A certain man by the name of Simon of Cyrene, the father of Alexander and Rufus, was passing by on his way in from the country, and they forced him to carry the cross.

(Mark 15:21 NIV)

Mark wrote that "they forced him." Wow. This man was simply passing by. In other words, this was not part of his day. This interaction wasn't on his agenda for the morning.

Simon was from Africa and had come in from his country and was just passing by. He wasn't there for Jesus. He was most likely a Jew coming in to celebrate Passover and handle some business, and then return to his way of life. I can imagine this was an embarrassing moment for Simon. Why? Because Simon knew he would be associated with this man.

We live in a day and age where everyone is trying to be associated with everyone.

Ever have a coworker, pastor, or friend who tried to name-drop every-one they know? I call it "humble bragging." People do it all the time on social media—through their posts or Instagram stories—and they want you to buy into the idea that they are a "somebody" because of who they are associated with.

The opposite can also be true. It's amazing how fast people are ready to cut ties with someone when it comes to compromising their brand or reputation.

For example, an athlete can be loved by millions of people and have dozens of endorsements. But the moment something goes wrong, every-one runs for the hills. Why? Because people fear being associated with imperfect people.

We are so image conscience that we identify identity by association.

[As followers of Jesus we are called to serve, love, and pour our lives into everybody. That means the poor and the rich, those who are in need on the streets and those who are celebrities. We are all called to love the unlovable and raise our voice for the voiceless. We are called to fight for injustice and stand for those who can't stand for themselves.] At VIVE Culture, we tell our teams that if someone is in front of us, we are going to find a way to serve them.

There are no categories at VIVE Culture. Every story matters.

We've seen past generations turn their backs on the world because of guilt by association. I'm so thankful we are seeing a shift; churches all over the world are full of believers running toward the world. It doesn't matter if you are rich or poor, if you are a model citizen, or have lots of baggage; our doors are open so people find Jesus.

Simon was like many of us. Simon didn't want to be put in the sinner's category. This would have been very embarrassing.

[What an extreme word picture Jesus is trying to get across to us today. Followship starts with unexpected interruptions that change the course of our lives. What started out as an interruption to Simon's regularly scheduled program eventually began to awaken something in him that he never knew was missing. It began to dawn on him that this was not a normal man.]

Simon's life was interrupted by what we now know is a picture of the gospel. It's an incredible picture of grace. It is a call to a life of servanthood. It is a life that requires giving everything.

I don't know about you, but I wasn't born looking for Jesus.

I get so fired up when I watch religious people looking down on other people, as if they popped out of the womb singing worship songs and living on purpose *with* a purpose.

Stop it. If you want to see VIVE Culture get fired up, we will unapologetically fight for every single person's right to have a place at the feet of Jesus. Every color, race, background, and social class. We will fight to create a culture where people can belong before they even believe. We are a church that is passionate about reaching people with the hope of the gospel. We are committed to serving our city and inviting them to feel like they are part of a family even before they choose to follow Jesus.

I was like Simon. I was *that* guy! I was a young man who had one thing on his mind . . . me. I was looking out for me and was doing whatever I could to lift myself up. I was trying to do everything I could not to serve people.

I was running from the call God had on my life. If I'm being completely vulnerable, people bothered me. I wasn't a people person. I tried to stay out of the way, kept my head down, and lived my own life.

Simon thought he was being inconvenienced and bothered. But what he didn't know yet was that he was given one of the highest privileges in human history. Simon had the privilege and honor of being the only man to carry the cross of the Savior of the world.

So many people are looking for titles.

How about picking up a towel and serving someone?

How about serving in such an extravagant way that it compels those who are far from God to discover what it means to be part of something bigger than themselves?

How about giving in such a generous way with no strings attached just to be a blessing?

How about loving someone without expecting anything in return?

Simon thought that carrying the cross from Jesus was an interruption, but instead it became his mark in history. How? Through serving. Isn't this what Jesus modeled for us over two thousand years ago?

For God so loved the world that he gave his one and only Son, that whoever believes in him shall not perish but have eternal life.

(John 3:16)

That verse does not say that God so loved the world that *we* gave. It says that God so loved the world that He gave. My favorite part of that verse is that He came for the "whosoevers." Next, consider what Matthew wrote:

Just as the Son of Man did not come to be served, but to serve, and to give his life as a ransom for many.

(Matthew 20:28)

Aren't you thankful for what Jesus did? If we are really going to reflect Jesus, it isn't in pursuing a life of leadership, but rather a life of servanthood. Serving paves the way for influence. Followship opens up the door to our destiny.

Jesus calls you and me to this amazing invitation of servanthood despite our imperfections. Take a deep breath. That is so freeing. He's not asking us to get cleaned up first.

It was our sin that caused Jesus to walk that road of suffering. We had a debt we could not pay, but Jesus paid that debt—a debt He did not owe—so we could be saved.

I'm so grateful that Jesus was willing to walk that road for you and me. Jesus turned the worst ending and what we were destined for into the greatest ending because of that cross.

Jesus went all in for you and me. Now He's asking you to go all in with the life He's entrusted to you. The cross is a constant reminder that He is for you, with you, believes in you, and is pursuing you even before you even decided to choose to follow Him. That's the beauty of grace. Jesus isn't like me with my wife and daughters, grossed out with certain things and trying to put up boundaries.

Instead, He wants you to run toward Him and come just as you are. He wants your entire heart.

How would you serve others today if you knew you were totally loved, fully forgiven, and empowered by God's Spirit?

Live that way because you are!

Whoever goes all in for the sake of Jesus will find life. Not only did Simon find life but so did his sons and family.

Two other men are mentioned later on in the New Testament, Alexander and a man named Rufus. They show up in the early church writings. Many believe these men were Simon's sons who ended up following Jesus and became missionaries because of the example of Simon leading his family.

Men, you have no idea the authority that has been placed on your life to lead your home to serve Jesus. The biggest thing we will stand before God on is not how much we saved in our 401K. Jesus won't ask how big our house was or how many vacations we took our families on. One day we will stand before God and He will ask us how we led our homes.

Did we teach our kids to follow Jesus by our example? At VIVE Culture, we have such a passion to reach the men in our generation because we believe if we can reach the man, we can reach the entire home. We will talk about that later on in the book, but there is a call in this generation for men to start leading their families through servanthood.

This way of living I'm talking about is a destiny changer. And it demands that we go all in.

Author and speaker Francis Chan once said, "Lukewarm people do not live by faith; their lives are structured so that they don't have to."

This is what God says—the God who builds a road right through the ocean, who carves a path through pounding waves: "Forget about what's happened; don't keep going over old history. Be alert, be present. I'm about to do something brand-new. It's bursting out! Don't you see it? There it is! I'm making a road through the desert, rivers in the badlands."

(Isaiah 43:16–21 MSG)

There are moments in life where you have to burn the ships.

[What I mean by that is you have to eliminate the possibility of sailing back to that old you, that old mentality, that old way of reacting, or that old way you use to treat your spouse. You have to choose to burn the ships of guilt, shame, gossip, being sarcastic, being promiscuous, or being overly scheduled where there's no time for unexpected interruptions.]

When you burn the ships you actually are free to pursue a life that is focused on others. When you don't, you begin to be so self-consumed that you can't think of anything else but yourself.

We see it all the time.

[Think about this for a moment. How can one person can be full of hope in the middle of watching their young child go through chemotherapy, and another be full of complaints about their kids' busy schedules—kids who are completely healthy? How can one person be barely making it financially and not know how they are going to pay the bills but still be full of generosity, while another person with money in the bank and a great job be constantly telling people how poor they are? How can a couple be full of gratitude, even though they can't conceive a child, while another couple who are blessed with kids seems to be constantly annoyed about how little sleep they are getting?

It's all about perspective.]

I am still working through trying to die to self every day and trying my best to pursue a life of servanthood. I know I'm not where I want to be yet, but thank God I'm not where I used to be, or where I should be if not for His grace. We are all a work in progress. The good news for your life today is that we can live a life fully devoted to following Jesus and serving others despite our shortcomings.

But we must create space in our lives for unexpected interruptions. We have to give some breathing room to our calendars for God to use us to serve a cause bigger than our own.

At VIVE, we are full of people that get to serve our city. We don't *have* to. We *get* to. It is a completely different feeling when you are surrounded by men, women, singles, teens, and families who show up every week and say, "I can't believe we get to do this."

The greatest and highest privilege of our lives is to walk with Jesus, carry our cross, and have a front-row seat in seeing the gospel impact our generation. In a generation that is full of options and things focused on living for self, there is a generation rising up and saying, "Ride or die . . . I'm all in."

I believe with all of my heart that this is the Jesus generation.

We are seeing a generation that is committed to serving the whosoevers. We don't care if you live in a million-dollar home or if you are living in a box on the streets. We consider every person who stands in front of us a celebrity.

What story are you going to tell with the life you are living? I don't know about you but I want to be like Simon where my kids and grandkids find life, hope, and purpose because of decisions we made to follow Jesus and serve people. Kids are smart. They know when your heart's not into something. Body language and countenance speak louder than words.

You might be reading this book and asking yourself: *how I can be this excited to serve others?*

The answer is because it's not religion that has our attention. It's about a relationship.

[Religious people obey God to get things. Gospel people obey God to get God.] It's an awakening to the Savior of all mankind. I pray that the highlight of our lives is to be identified with Jesus. And when we are identified with Him we begin to reflect Him, which is a life of servanthood.

When we are consumed with being identified with Him, we can't help but run to our city and serve in any way we can.

> We serve with our time.
> We serve with our finances.
> We serve with our gifts.
> We serve with our words.
> What a privilege!

I'm sure if we could sit across the table from Simon today, he wouldn't complain about how bloody his back got from Jesus' blood, or how many splinters he got in his shoulders from carrying that old piece of wood. Knowing what we know now, I'm sure he would be like, "I wasn't looking for it, I didn't ask for it, I wasn't in the mood for it, and I didn't have time for it. But the more I carried that cross and the further we went down that road, the more I realized I'm the most privileged person in human history." I have tears just thinking of that.

By the end of this book, I pray we can see that we are the most privileged people in history to carry His Name to every corner of the planet. That's the kind of people we are striving to be in our city. Serving isn't what we do. Serving is who we are. — MAKE SERVING PART OF WHO YOU ARE

What would your church look like if every person who identified themselves with your community said, "I'm all in. I don't need a title. I don't need a paycheck. I just want to be part of something bigger than myself."

Jesus is waiting for you to answer the call to serve your city. He is waiting for you to step up and commit to a life to serve your family.

Jesus sent His twelve harvest hands out with this charge: "Don't begin by traveling to some far-off place to convert unbelievers. And don't try to be dramatic by tackling some public enemy. Go to the lost, confused people right here in the neighborhood. *(In other words, run to your city.)* Tell them that the kingdom is here. Bring health to the sick. Raise the dead. Touch the untouchables. Kick out the demons. You have been treated generously, so live generously. Don't think you have to put on a campaign before you start. You don't need a lot of equipment. You are the equipment. If you don't go all the way with me, through thick and thin, you don't deserve me. If your first concern is to look after yourself, you'll never find yourself. But if you forget about yourself and look to me, you'll find both yourself and me."]

(Portions of Matthew 10 MSG)

The best way to change the world is to allow the Holy Spirit to continually change you. Changed people, change people. When our lives have been radically changed we can take that same grace into our neighborhoods to help others discover Jesus by inviting them into this grace life that we know. The more we understand this grace, the more we will become the least offended people on the planet and extend so much more grace to others.

[The best promotion of the gospel is not a website or campaign slogan. It's a changed life. It needs no promotion.]

Jesus picked people with issues and called them to a life of servanthood. Moses had anger issues. David committed adultery with Bathsheba and murdered her husband Uriah. Rahab was a prostitute. Jonah was a racist and a hyper-nationalist. Peter had all sorts of issues. Thomas doubted. Paul killed Christians. But still, God promoted each to a life of servanthood. *Jesus will use your mess as your message*

If Jesus could use them, He can use us too!

Jesus took the V.I.P. rope down and said the whosoevers would become His agents of grace.

This is our God. You have everything you need. [You may feel like your boat is sinking. I'm here to tell you Jesus never promised He'd save your boat. But He did promise He'd save you. Sometimes the best thing that can happen in our lives is for our boats to sink so we are awakened to what He really has for us.]

The best thing God did for me was to allow my boat to sink so He could show me a new way of leading . . . and that's through serving. I want this for me and I want this for you as well.

2

the underdog story

Americans are no strangers to rivalry. We thrive on it. We are intrigued by it. We give millions of dollars to it. I enjoy college sports because of the fans, but I'm a die-hard pro sports fan. There's nothing like the best athletes in the world going head-to-head with one another. I love my Chicago teams. The Chicago Bears, Bulls, Blackhawks, and White Sox have my heart. I don't just cheer for them—I represent them. I follow them even during the off-season. I'm invested.

My favorite pro sport is the NBA. Some of the most talented and athletic athletes of our time are in that league. There has never been a better time to be an NBA fan than right now. I grew up a Chicago Bulls fan. I love them with all my heart. I know it has been a shaky decade for my team, but every season I believe we have a shot to compete.

I'd be lying, though, if I didn't admit that I miss the days when I would watch Michael Jordan take on the entire league. It's a different NBA today than what it used to be. Jordan wasn't trying to join a super team. He was the super team. He wasn't trying to team up with his friends. He was trying to destroy them.

In that time in history, every team had a rivalry with my Bulls. Whether they admitted it or not, everyone wanted to be like Mike. Every young basketball player in the world watched the VHS movie called Michael Jordan's Playground. Michael Jordan inspired all of us talking about the highs and lows of his basketball career. Everyone I knew wanted to be like MJ. I would watch that movie and then go outside and try to imitate him.

My little brother, Steven, is one of my best friends. He and I shared a room growing up. The perk of sharing a room with one of your brothers is you spend a lot of time together. I loved hanging out with him because we both shared the same passion for sports. We didn't just like sports—we were obsessed with them. He and I would grab the boom box, pop in the Bulls soundtrack cassette tape, and play ball for hours. We would act like the crowds were cheering for us as we went head-to-head. He loved the New York Knicks, which he still loves, and I was the star guard on the Chicago Bulls.

Steven could hold his own—but we both knew that basketball was something he could never really beat me in. In football, I didn't have a chance. Of course, I could play pretty well, but he was clearly more gifted in football than I was. He was so gifted that he even went on to play in college. I was so proud of him. But in hoops, I owned him.

Jordan made playing with your tongue hanging out cool. I tried to dress like him, play like him, and chew gum like him. I love the rivals in sports.

When I think about rivals in the Bible there's one story that comes to mind and that's David and Goliath. I want to look at this story that was bigger than the Los Angeles Lakers versus the Chicago Bulls. This rival was one of the most epic showdowns in history. In fact, we are still talking about this battle centuries later. It was the Israelites versus the Philistines.

Even if you haven't grown up inside the walls of a church, chances are you have heard the story of David and Goliath. This man David was an incredible historic figure. We know more about David than almost any other man in history.

The part of the story we are going to unpack together isn't simply about a young shepherd boy killing a mean old giant. The true meaning of the story all started because of one man's willingness to serve.

Let me set the stage for you. An epic battle was about to begin. Israel's army waited on one hill; on the other, the Philistine army. The Philistines gathered their army for war. The Philistines stem from the days in Genesis and the Egyptian people. A key to their dominance was in their more advanced material culture. While the Israelites still practiced Bronze Age skills, the Philistines had advanced to an Iron Age culture, making them nearly invincible on the battlefield. We learn from reading Scripture that the children of Israel had no spears or swords. They fought with weapons like axes and sickles.

Saul, who was king at the time, could only muster up two swords. One was for him, and one was for his son, Jonathan. That would be a great disadvantage when going against a juggernaut like the Philistines.

Not only were the Philistines physically intimidating, but they also fought with swords, spears, and chariots made of iron, which made them impossible to conquer. The Philistines had no intention of trying to negotiate peace with the children of Israel. They were there for war. The lines were drawn.

The Philistines occupied one hill and the Israelites another, with the valley between them.

(1 Samuel 17:3)

No one was in the valley. This tells me the lines had been drawn and there was no one "on the fence" as to whose side they were on. In this rivalry, you were either on one side or the other. There was no middle ground.

The Philistines were an influential people group that made it their mission in life to dominate everyone who didn't line up with their way of life. They built five gigantic cities whose armies caused their enemies to tremble with fear. They were merciless. They were ruthless warriors, ready to wipe Israel off of the planet once and for all.

The Philistines planned on everything you could think of, except for one unknown shepherd boy named David. When you study David's life, you begin to realize he was no different than you or me. He was human and flawed. He struggled, failed, and prevailed just like us. But God had a plan for his life that he would strategically weave into the fabric of His story. This insignificant, unknown teenager was chosen by God even when his own family didn't see much in him.

SEEING POTENTIAL IN PEOPLE

King Saul led Israel during a difficult time in history. During that time, there was a prophet named Samuel who was a spokesman for God. During the reign of King Saul, he had begun to make so many bad decisions and disobeyed God so many times that God finally had enough.

> Samuel continued, "You may not think you're very important, but the Lord chose you to be king, and you are in charge of the tribes of Israel. When the Lord sent you on this mission, he told you to wipe out those worthless Amalekites. Why didn't you listen to the Lord?"
>
> (1 Samuel 15:17–19a CEV)

King Saul knew that he had disobeyed God and Samuel told him he would no longer be king. It's interesting that King Saul was stripped of his anointing as king, but still held the royal title.

God had enough. He sent the prophet Samuel on a mission to find a person He could trust to rise up and lead His nation forward. He was looking for a very specific character trait in someone. If you or I were looking for someone, I'd image we'd look for someone similar to Goliath. If we were picking teams on the blacktop, we would start off picking the biggest, strongest, and most gifted to be on our team.

[God wasn't looking for the most gifted. He was looking for someone who was faithful.]King Saul was all about himself, so much so that even after he was told he would be replaced, instead of having a change of heart, King Saul desired to kill anyone who would try and dethrone him.

Imagine that. King Saul didn't earn his position or any talents he possessed. He was given them. And somehow he felt entitled to kill anyone who threatened the throne he was entrusted with. It's funny how that works.

God gave the prophet Samuel clear instructions to go to a man named Jesse in Bethlehem and anoint one of his sons as Israel's next king:

> But Samuel said, "How can I go? If Saul hears about it, he will kill me." The Lord said, "Take a heifer with you and say, 'I have come to sacrifice to the Lord.' Invite Jesse to the sacrifice, and I will show you what to do. You are to anoint for me the one I indicate."

> (1 Samuel 16:2–3)

Even Samuel, as respected as he was, feared for his life. That tells us that King Saul put everyone on notice that he wasn't giving up his seat without a fight. Despite his fears, Samuel obeyed God. And when Samuel arrived into town, he asked Jesse to bring his sons to a sacrifice that Samuel would prepare for them.

I wish I were there in that house when he asked to meet Jesse's sons. Can you imagine if someone came to your house unexpectedly and said that one of your kids was chosen to be the next president of the United States?

As parents, if we heard that, we'd cross some of our kids off the list right away. You know what I'm talking about. If someone said one of your kids was going to be the next president, you would eliminate the children who have trouble tying their shoes.

It's easy to judge what Jesse was about to do, but parents know there are some things their kids just won't be able to do. Is that okay to say in this day and age? I know we live in a society where everyone gets a participation trophy, but I'm an old-school parent. I am trying to set my kids up for real life.

For example, my fourth born, Brooklyn Hope, is gifted in so many things. But she can't dribble a basketball to save her life. It's unbelievable. I can't believe she even has the same DNA as my wife and me when she's trying to dribble.

It's almost shocking how uncoordinated she is. But Brooklyn thinks it's hilarious. If you came up to me and said, "One of your kids will get a full-ride scholarship to play at UNC on a basketball scholarship," I would cross her right off the list. She would be lucky to last a season in a paid league. Brooklyn is gifted in many things. She is one of the funniest, most loving girls I've ever known—but dribbling a basketball is not one of her skill sets. And the truth is, she doesn't care about sports. Ballet or dance is where she shines and comes to life.

The point is, as much potential as we see in our kids, there are certain things we know they will never be able to do.

I don't know everything about Jesse, but one thing is clear: he didn't see potential in David. Jesse brought the sons to the anointing ceremony that he saw potential in. This is a big moment as a parent. This is that moment where you get out your phone and you Instagram a story of how great of a parent you are. It's the moment you let the world know that your kid is going to be the next king. Consider this scene:

Jesse had seven of his sons pass before Samuel, but Samuel said to him, "The Lord has not chosen these." So he asked Jesse, "Are these all the sons you have?" "There is still the youngest," Jesse answered. "He is tending the sheep."

(1 Samuel 16:10–11)

Can we push the pause button for a second? You mean to tell me this man had every one of his kids come to the ceremony but left the youngest of the family in the fields tending sheep? Did this father have no heart? I find this incredibly sad and humorous at the same time.

He's the kind of father that would say, "You know what, I've heard you read out loud and Stanford just isn't in the cards for you, son."

Jesse is harsh. He had all his sons come meet Samuel except for the baby of the family. I'm sure Samuel was expecting God to pick the best looking and the most gifted. It makes sense. That's human nature. However, God has something else in mind:

But the Lord said to Samuel, "Do not consider his appearance or his height, for I have rejected him. The Lord does not look at the things people look at. People look at the outward appearance, but the Lord looks at the heart."

(1 Samuel 16:7)

God was looking for a specific quality . . . a servant's heart.

You can imagine their surprise when none of the sons were chosen who passed before Samuel. Samuel was confused. Let's revisit this section of Scripture again:

So he asked Jesse, "Are these all the sons you have?" "There is still the youngest," Jesse answered. "He is tending the sheep." Samuel said, "Send for him; we will not sit down until he arrives."

(1 Samuel 16:11)

[As funny as this is to read, in real life it's all too common with parents. Every single one of our kids are a gift from God and we have no idea the potential He has deposited inside of them if we would just call it out in them.]

David was left alone in the fields tending the sheep. In other words, he was faithfully serving in an unseen place. I can't imagine what David was going through. If you want to talk about someone who had every right to have identity issues, it's David. If you want to talk about a teenager who really had a reason to feel depressed, it's this young man.

David's own father didn't see potential in him. I can't imagine what David was thinking when he was asked to meet Samuel.

"Me? I'm a nobody. I'm just a shepherd boy," he must have thought.

I wonder how many times he had those words spoken over his life to the point where he started to believe it. I wonder how many times his brothers passed by the fields making fun of him reminding him that he was a nobody. A shepherd boy in those days would never dream there would be more to his life than guarding the sheep.

David was the grunt work kid. He was the kid who did all the jobs that were beneath everyone else. And he was out watching the sheep when he received the call:

> So Jesse sent for him and had him brought in. He was glowing with health and had a fine appearance and handsome features. Then the Lord said, "Rise and anoint him; this is the one." So Samuel took the horn of oil and anointed him in the presence of his brothers, and from that day on the Spirit of the Lord came powerfully upon David. Samuel then went to Ramah.
>
> (1 Samuel 16:12–13)

There are certain words in this story that always jump out at me. How could David be glowing in health serving in the fields? Wouldn't he have come in annoyed? Wouldn't David have come in with a chip on his shoulder as the victim? If we are honest with ourselves, most of us would have come in full of hopelessness.

Being a shepherd in those days was one of the worst jobs you could be asked to do. It was one of the lowest tasks given to someone. It was the job given to a person with no potential. Can you imagine how long the days were or how cold the nights would get watching sheep? Can you imagine how lonely David must have felt?

But David came in "glowing in health" after serving in the fields.

This teenager was special.

David had every right to show up angry. He was left out of the meeting. His own father didn't think enough of him to even invite him to the table. However, David had a different spirit. David chose to keep his spirit healthy.

David was the one Samuel was looking for. With the horn of oil, Samuel anointed David as the next king of Israel. When I read the Bible, I see things a little differently. Most people focus on what David must have been feeling. For me, I think it's amazing that this happened in front of his family that left him out of the party. Now that's the justice side of me that always comes out. I love that Samuel performed this ceremony in front of David's brothers who thought just as little of him as Jesse did.

The horn of oil that Samuel used to anoint David as the next king is a symbol of the Holy Spirit in the New Testament. David is literally anointed with the Holy Spirit to be the next king to serve his generation.

The pathway to leadership didn't come from a title, or whom David knew, but rather it came through servanthood.

WILLING TO DO WHATEVER IT TAKES

I love having a big family. It's always been a dream for us to have a house full of kids. But it can be a challenge at times. We are constantly trying to teach our kids to work hard because life doesn't owe you anything, and also how valuable it is to serve one another.

As humans, we are not born selfless. We are born *selfish*. We can't escape it. Even as adults, we never outgrow it. It's a constant battle to learn how to put others first and carry a spirit of servanthood.

For some reason God chose to bless our home with six strong-willed kids. I mean, God couldn't give a brotha a break and give me one kid with no ambitions or opinions in life? All my kids have strong personalities to some extent, but my oldest daughter Kaitlyn who is eleven, and my fifth born London, who is five, got a double-dose of that gene. They are as Type-A as they come.

It's hilarious, and exhausting at times, to watch those two try and lead one another. It's like watching two bulls going head-to-head. They both hate being led and it is like pulling teeth to get them to serve one another. They want to be in charge.

I remember one Friday night they were going back and forth as to who was going to pick the movie for family movie night. If you are a parent, you know the littlest thing with your kids can become a big thing in a moment's notice.

My other four kids didn't seem to care what movie they watched. Makayla was making everyone popcorn, Riley was getting the pillows, and

Brooklyn was taking care of Jude—but Kaitlyn and London were battling for who was going to pick the movie.

I know perfect parents stop things quick before they get out of control but we are not perfect parents. In most cases we try and stop things before they escalate but there are moments when Alicia and I just let things go for our own entertainment. Please don't judge us for that. Sometimes you just have to let things go and watch your kids work issues out themselves.

Kaitlyn is the typical oldest child. She is responsible, driven, competitive, and wants all her siblings to fall in line. She's such a gift to our house. London is a gift as well and she is no pushover. She was born a fighter. London Joy is our NICU baby. She was born with doctors poking her with needles in her feet, scalp, and belly button. We thought we could potentially lose her the first week of her life if things didn't turn around.

Trust me, London can take care of herself. So sadly, I was kind of enjoying seeing my eleven and five-year-old going head-to-head. What really made Kaitlyn mad wasn't so much that London wanted to pick the movie, but the fact that she didn't want *Kaitlyn* to pick it.

Kaitlyn was trying to be logical about it. London was standing on principal. She wanted to be in charge and was letting Kaitlyn know that she wasn't surrendering to her ideas. Even if London liked the movie Kaitlyn picked, she was stubborn enough to pass on it. I could see it was really starting to upset Kaitlyn.

I pulled Kaitlyn aside and asked her why she was so upset.

"She just won't listen to what I say. It's not fair. I'm the oldest so she needs to just be quiet and do whatever I say," Kaitlyn said.

She had a point. She was the oldest and she could impose her will on London if she really wanted to. Of course, I could pull the trump card at any time and shut both of them down, but then again, what would that really be teaching them about serving one another? Instead, I posed a different question to her.

"Kaitlyn, what does being a great leader mean to you?" I asked.

Of course, Kaitlyn being the person that she is had a quick and direct answer for me. "It means that I'm in charge and everyone has to listen to me," she said with a strong voice.

She wasn't totally wrong. When you are in charge, people do have to listen to you. But that wasn't the question. The question was, what does being a *great leader* mean?

What I tried to teach her in that moment was if she wanted to be the best leader that she could be, she would have to learn how to follow first. Great leaders do whatever it takes to serve others. It's not about titles. I told her that if she wanted to be a great leader, she had to learn to serve others.

I would love to tell you that Kaitlyn left with this new revelation that radically changed the course of her life. That didn't happen. As you can imagine, at the moment that little lesson didn't go over exactly the way I hoped. It led to a longer conversation about who was right and who was wrong. If you have daughters, you know how those conversations can go at times. But at least it was a teaching moment to build on.

If my daughters want to be great moms someday to their kids, it starts by learning how to serve their siblings. If my sons want to be great husbands, it starts by them learning how to serve their mom. I want my kids to serve so generously that they will do whatever it takes to serve others.

It's about faithfulness. Can we be trusted with things that no one else wants to do? David was one of those individuals. He came from a big family and he was willing to do whatever was asked of him. And every single thing he was asked to do was building his character for something greater to come.

SERVING IS AN HONOR

David was now the next anointed king of Israel. And what happens next? Nothing.

David left that ceremony and went right back to serving his father's house. I can relate in some ways. When God called my wife and me to lead a church when we were first married, nothing immediately changed. We went right back to the jobs we were serving in. We didn't tell a soul what

God spoke to us. We just kept it in our hearts until it was time and decided to keep serving whatever mission was put in front of us.

Maybe you can relate to that too in your own personal way.

David didn't automatically move into the palace. Instead, he went right back to the fields where he would be left all alone. Now during that same time, this epic battle between Israel and the Philistines was about to come to a head. It became so real that all of Jesse's sons were sent off to fight in this battle. Clearly David wasn't identified as a warrior, because he wasn't asked to go fight.

> Now Jesse said to his son David, "Take this ephah of roasted grain and these ten loaves of bread for your brothers and hurry to their camp. Take along these ten cheeses to the commander of their unit. See how your brothers are and bring back some assurance from them. They are with Saul and all the men of Israel in the Valley of Elah, fighting against the Philistines."

> (1 Samuel 17:17–19)

I love the picture of honoring leadership in these verses.

[Honor is something that has become a lost value in our society. Everyone wants to be served—and we won't show anyone honor if we think they don't deserve it. However, I believe there is a special blessing on individual hearts and churches that embrace a spirit of honor.]

We see all throughout the Bible that God shows favor to those who choose to honor others. You don't have to respect a person to show them honor.

In those verses that we just read, Jesse not only honored his sons by sending them food, but he also sent along food to the commander of their units as well. That is an intentional display of honoring leadership that is so important to our spiritual walk. Jesse didn't just send enough food for his kids, but for his leaders, too.

But whom did he ask to deliver the food? David. Remember, David was the anointed king. Jesse knew this. All of his brothers knew this. He was no longer a scrub. David was anointed by God to be the future king of Israel. If anyone had a right to sit back and demand to be served, it would have been David.

In that day and age, kings were gods. Think about if you or I were anointed to be the future king or queen. I wonder: How many of us would have the character to keep it quiet and go back to serving our boss?

David could have said, "Pops look, I'm the king now. I don't do this cheese thing. I'm going to rule the world and rule over you. I paid my dues. It's time for me to be served. In fact, my brothers should be bringing me bread."

David didn't respond like that because David had a different spirit:

Early in the morning David left the flock in the care of a shepherd, loaded up and set out, as Jesse had directed. He reached the camp as the army was going out to its battle positions, shouting the war cry.

(1 Samuel 17:20)

Instead of telling everyone how gifted he was, David humbly submitted himself to his father to serve. David was willing to follow, even though he knew he was called to lead. David wasn't sitting back gloating and he wasn't kicking his feet up waiting for his glorious reign as king. He continued to do what he had always had done . . . serve.

David was given an assignment and humbly accepted it. The assignment wasn't sexy and it wasn't fun. And because he was willing to embrace this small, insignificant opportunity to serve his brothers and leaders, he was then placed in the exact spot where God wanted him to be.

Think about this for a moment. David was so faithful and trustworthy that he didn't just abandon the sheep he cared for. He left them with another shepherd to look after. If you want to see what type of leader someone will be, watch that person care for something they don't own.

Watch them serve and care for a vision that isn't their own. If you want to know what a person is really like, watch them serve someone who can't do another thing for them. David was a skilled warrior who learned how to build his skill set through serving.

I heard it once said that a smooth sea never produced a skillful sailor. That's so true. Through serving, David realized he had what it took to kill a bear and a lion. He sharpened his skills through a life of servanthood.

The only reason David was ready to walk in his destiny is because he was willing to honor the process of serving in unseen places.

David did what he was asked to do. When he arrived on the scene of the battle that was about to take place, David wasn't prepared for what he was about to see. On one side of the hill stood the great Philistines, taunting and speaking against the God of Israel, and on the other side of the hill Israel's soldiers were hiding in their tents, full of fear.

THERE'S A TIME TO PLAN AND A TIME TO ACT

David thought he was just there to deliver food. That was what was asked of him. But he couldn't shake what he was seeing. There is such a difference between a person who shows up to get the task asked of them done and the person who sees the need and finds solutions to make it better.

People ask me all the time: [What do I look for in a great leader? I think they are surprised by my answer. One of the things I look for is someone's ability to see a need and take action. I think if you aren't scared every now and then you aren't really living by faith. But fear doesn't have to cripple you. Sometimes something is stirred so greatly in you that you're ready to jump in and do something.]

I love telling the story of why we planted VIVE Culture. We didn't plant our church because we were bored at the church we were serving in. We loved the church we were serving in at the time. We were serving at a great church in Lee's Summit, Missouri, and loved the people with all of our hearts. We loved our pastors and the leadership there, and we were about to move into a brand-new 32,000-square-foot facility. We had no reason to leave.

However, we couldn't shake the call God placed on our hearts when we were first married, no matter how hard we tried. Believe me, I tried to ignore it. I tried to talk myself out of it. I tried to talk God out of it but for some reason it would never leave us.

In 2010, I was hired at Eagle Creek Church to be the creative arts pastor. We came in during a rough season the church was walking through. By God's grace He saw us through and we began to see God move in some amazing ways. During that time of growth, the leadership knew we were outgrowing the space we were renting and that it was time to build. So they started a building campaign that turned into three building campaigns. At the same time, we launched two other locations, we opened up a Café venue as an overflow room, I began to oversee more areas for the church, and we were working on building plans for the new property. It was crazy season to say the least. In the seven years that I served on staff there, we experienced a 300 percent growth rate. It was amazing to be a tiny part of that season in that church's history.

In the meantime, God was working on my heart in so many areas. I have to be honest: there were many times I wanted to quit. I can't tell you how many times on the way home from a long day I asked God to be released to run with the vision in my own heart. I had such a specific vision for the church God had in mind for us to lead, and I couldn't do that in the position I was in.

Often, people hear a story like that and instantly think there was something wrong or negative with the church. However, it had absolutely nothing to do with the leadership we were serving under. We had and continue to have a great relationship with the lead pastors of that church and their entire leadership board.

Eagle Creek Church was our sending church for VIVE Culture; they commissioned us, covered our salary as we planted, and they are one of the biggest reasons VIVE was able to launch the way that we did. We couldn't have done it without our Eagle Creek family behind us.

I know that's rare to hear, but it was such an honor to serve our pastors and their vision. It had nothing to do with them. It had everything to do with the calling on our lives and what God was doing in my heart. God wired my wife and me to lead a certain way and to build teams a certain way, and I felt like I was missing my chance to fulfill that call.

I remember one morning I was praying about the church I felt God had for us, and God spoke so gently to my heart. It was so clear that He wanted us to serve our pastors and see them through these building campaigns we were in the middle of. I went home that day and told my wife what I felt God was speaking to us and we decided that we were going to honor the process and give everything we had to see our church's vision become a reality. I wanted my pastor to feel like I was so loyal to his vision that I could help absorb a lot of the pressure and responsibility that was on his shoulders.

I felt a clear assignment to make sure that the church he was called to lead was able to break ground on their new property. I knew that once they broke ground, they would be set up for decades to impact their community. I knew I was helping them get into a permanent building my family would never be in.

It's so funny how God's timing works because when we were in Florida on vacation, I received a text from our lead pastor telling us that they signed the loan to break ground on their new building. An hour later our landlord texted us to tell us he was selling the house we had lived in for the past five years.

Not to mention that same day, our sixth born, Jude Benjamin, started walking for the first time. Talk about a day full of emotions. It was time to move forward.

[I want to tell you that the moment we made that decision to go all in and serve as if it was our own vision, it changed everything. I began to learn things about pastoring I would have never learned if I resisted serving.] My former pastor entrusted me with more and allowed me to be his right-hand man and learn things about how to run a multi-site church that I would have never learned anywhere else. I believe he did this because over time he knew he could trust me to care for this vision that God placed in his heart as much as I would care for my own vision.

As time went on, God started to surround my wife and I with such gifted, fun, passionate team members in our areas of ministry that became like family to us. We began to do life together and just loved being in ministry together.

Many of those same people moved forward with us to plant VIVE Culture because great teams find ways to stay together.

You see, so many churches around the world have had the same core team members for decades. When you sit down and ask them if it gets old I'm stunned when they say it only gets better! Longevity is such a gift to a local church when you are serving under a leadership that you love being around.

I can honestly say I will never forget the look on our former pastors' faces when they were standing on their new land during the ground breaking service. The joy on their faces when their family dug that shovel into the ground and threw the dirt into the air was something I'll never forget.

When that happened, I knew the time had finally come for us to answer the call to lead our own church with the team He was preparing for us.

God was so faithful during that transition season. After the ground breaking service, I told our pastor what God was doing in our hearts and he wasn't surprised. Apparently he knew it was coming for a few years. He couldn't have been more supportive. I was in tears not only because I loved him and our church, but also because of the journey God was taking me on.

I couldn't believe that after all these years, it was finally time to answer the call that He planted in our hearts in San Diego.

God honored our family by allowing us to be Eagle Creek Church's first official church plant.

I think that says more about how much we loved one another than anything else.

We will always be incredibly grateful for the years we spend serving under that leadership. Every life-change story and person impacted by the gospel Eagle Creek Church will have part in. They will always have a special place in our hearts.

So when we set out to plant VIVE Culture, we didn't know what city God wanted us to pour our lives into. So we prayed. And prayed. And yes, we prayed some more. We even brought our kids along for this decision. We do everything as a family. We had them pray with us and asked them what they were feeling. No matter what city we were talking about, nothing made our hearts come alive like when we talked about Kansas City.

We love it and our kids love being here! We decided that Kansas City was the city we were called to be in and the more we began to dig into the needs of Kansas City, our hearts knew we were in for the fight of our lives. Currently in Kansas City, 75 percent of the Kansas City Metro area are not Christians and do not attend a Jesus-church. It is ranked twenty-ninth in the nation in child wellbeing and ranks higher in indicators of divorce, domestic violence, and poverty.

Kansas City is the second out of the top ten metropolitan cities when it comes to human trafficking. It has more than 6,500 kids in the foster care system right now. As incredible as this city is, the underlining spirit of racism that still exists in our city is undeniable, but it's masked by zip codes, school systems, and sports programs.

VIVE Culture was birthed out of desperation to reach people who were far from God and lead them to experience new life in Jesus. The needs in our city are overwhelming. Where do you even start with stats like that?

My wife and I didn't have a marketing plan, a budget, a church building, or even a name at that time. We didn't even know if anyone would be crazy enough to want to join us and move forward with the vision we had for our city. We just knew God was up to something big and whatever it was we wanted in on it. We weren't okay with how the enemy of our souls was dominating our city.

We wanted VIVE to break the mold in our city!

We were ready to fight for it. We were ready to fight for every family who was missing out on this incredible grace. We were ready to fight for every story yet to be heard. We were ready to fight for every kid who is trapped in human slavery and every child who has to go to bed without a family to love them. We were ready to stand up for every person who has been a victim of domestic violence or racism. It wasn't enough to put on a Sunday experience. We wanted to be a church that was all about serving our city.

We were leaving a place that was about to move into an amazing new facility and start from ground zero. But the time for praying was over.

It was time to take action. The story of VIVE is really a story of a small team of people who took flight with the desire to foster a family of believers connected by a common faith, on a mission to amplify the Name of Jesus. Our heart is to lead a relational, refreshing, and relevant church that is in love with serving our city.

David found himself in a similar boat. He didn't get the blueprint of how his life was going to play out. He didn't know all the ins and outs of how to perfectly take down this giant. David's heart was so enraged by the injustice he was seeing that he couldn't stand by and do nothing.

[I know this is going to be hard to hear, but God's primary concern is not our safety or our comfort.

God's primary concern is that His glory and fame is proclaimed to every person so they can be invited into the same story that we are part of.]

David is my kind of guy. He's feisty. I love that about him. He doesn't go away. He is willing to fight for what he believes in. His gifts made room for him through a life of servanthood and now the moment has finally come for him to step into his destiny:

> David asked the men standing near him, "What will be done for the man who kills this Philistine and removes this disgrace from Israel? Who is this uncircumcised Philistine that he should defy the armies of the living God?"
>
> When Eliab, David's oldest brother, heard him speaking with the men, he burned with anger at him and asked, "Why have you come down here? And with whom did you leave those few sheep in the wilderness? I know how conceited you are and how wicked your heart is; you came down only to watch the battle."
>
> "Now what have I done?" said David. "Can't I even speak?" He then turned away to someone else and brought up the same matter, and the men answered him as before. What David said was overheard and reported to Saul, and Saul sent for him.
>
> (1 Samuel 17:26, 28–31)

We shouldn't be shocked that his brother, Eliab, responded this way. He was passed up to be king. It shows what little respect his family really had for David. When you say things like, "Those few sheep" it speaks of their lack of respect for them.

It's amazing what jealousy can do to a person's heart.

It would be like a well-known pastor asking another pastor, "How is that little church of yours doing?"

How insulting, right?

I've actually had that happen to me when we were planting VIVE. Trust me, it doesn't feel good.

David was the next king and yet his brothers still didn't see anything more in him than a shepherd boy. I love how David responded. He responded like any baby of the family.

"Now what have I done? Can't I even speak?"

That just sounds like something the baby of the family would say, doesn't it?

"Can't I do anything right? "

David wasn't going to let his brothers' insults silence him. David had a strength that everyone underestimated. He was willing to die for what he believed in.

That is a character trait in a leader that is attractional. David saw the injustice that was happening and he wasn't going to stand by and let it continue. It was time to take action. He led like a king before he had the title of king.

JUST BE YOURSELF

It's so easy to think we are not enough for the call that God places on our lives. But you will find over time that if you focus on who God's called you to be, you will be so much more fulfilled than if you try to be someone else. You are at your best when you embrace who you are.

We all go through phases in life. I've been through many of them. I went through a phase where I wanted to be The Fresh Prince of Bel Air. So I bought clothes that looked just like Will Smith and I tried to talk to girls like him. I went through a 2Pac phase. I can only imagine the laughs my mom and dad had over that one.

I even went through a phase early on in my ministry as a young pastor. I thought if I wanted to be a lead pastor someday, I had to preach like the other pastors I listened to. I didn't think that the way I communicated was enough. Let me tell you, it was a disaster. I wish they had the technology back then like they do today because I would replay it over and over again just to make fun of myself.

I went through a phase where I tried so hard to be like Andy Stanley, pastor of North Point Church. I tried to sit on a stool and sound intellectual when I preached. Unfortunately, I'm so passionate when I speak that I couldn't sit still. So I kept moving in my stool the whole time and it looked like I had to use the bathroom.

Then I went the opposite route and tried to be like T. D. Jakes, one of the greatest gospel preachers in our generation. I'm just going to leave that one alone. Let's just say I never tried that one again. It was a catastrophe.

I remember one time I even tried to be like this one theologian I was addicted to listening to as a young man. I wanted people to think I was smart and qualified. I can't stop laughing, even as I write this. I'm so embarrassed just thinking about that. I think I am the first pastor in history to put himself to sleep while preaching his own message. There was a point in that message where I thought to myself, "What in the world are you talking about?"

It was awful and I was so unfulfilled. I was wired to preach a certain way and lead my teams a certain way, but I didn't think it was enough. I was wired to lead relationally, but I thought if I wanted to lead an influential church, I had to lead by separating myself from those I led. I thought I had to be strong to be respected.

It wasn't until I was in my mid-twenties when one of my former pastors that I was serving with in California, who was leading a large and influential church, put his arm around me and said, "Brian, I don't want you to be me. I don't want you to be like anyone else. You have a special way of leading from your heart. You have a special way of leading your teams through relationships. That's what I love about you. You have it in you to be a lead pastor one day if you just lead and speak the way God wired you. Just be yourself. That will be enough. I believe in you and I'm proud of what you are doing around here."

He said that and walked away.

That was a defining moment for me. My pastor didn't even know what God had already called us to. We hadn't told a soul. It was just another confirmation. So from that moment on, I ditched the stools, I ignored the critics, and I began to learn how to be comfortable in my own skin. I started to build relationships with my team that looked more like a home than a company.

David had that defining moment.

David said to Saul, "Let no one lose heart on account of this Philistine; your servant will go and fight him." Saul replied, "You are not able to go out against this Philistine and fight him; you are only a young man, and he has been a warrior from his youth." But David said to Saul, "Your servant has been keeping his father's sheep. When a lion or a bear came and carried off a sheep from the flock, I went after it, struck it and rescued the sheep from its mouth. When it turned on me, I seized it by its hair, struck it and killed it. Your servant has killed both the lion and the bear; this uncircumcised Philistine will be like one of them, because he has defied the armies of the living God. The Lord who rescued me from the paw of the lion and the paw of the bear will rescue me from the hand of this Philistine."

[Saul said to David, "Go, and the Lord be with you."]

Then Saul dressed David in his own tunic. He put a coat of armor on him and a bronze helmet on his head. David fastened on his sword over the tunic and tried walking around, because he was not used to them.

"I cannot go in these," he said to Saul, "because I am not used to them." So he took them off. Then he took his staff in his hand, chose five smooth stones from the stream, put them in the pouch of his shepherd's bag and, with his sling in his hand, approached the Philistine.

(1 Samuel 17:32–40)

What an amazing picture of the spirit of servanthood. All the moments David served in unseen places and all the moments David was faithful to tasks asked of him had prepared him for this moment. I can't prove this, but if David would have taken shortcuts in the field, I don't think he would have been ready to face his Goliath. David was a worshiper. We know this by studying his life. I can picture David in the field with his instruments being captivated by the stars above him.

I imagine David wrote some of his best songs in the fields watching over those sheep. [The only way David could keep a healthy spirit doing meaningless tasks was by focusing his heart on God.] David could have let the lion or bear attack his flock and said, "These aren't my sheep. I'm just watching them for someone else. It's not worth giving my life to something so insignificant." But killing the lion and the bear gave him the experience he needed to be ready for this moment of truth. Thankfully, David was smart enough to know that he had to fight the way God wired him.

David was a leader worth following.

King Saul, not knowing that this was the future king of Israel, agreed to let David fight for Israel. King Saul was leading from the tent.

I find it funny that there were only two swords in the camp. One was for King Saul and the other was for his son, Jonathan, and neither one of them were planning on using them. I don't care how gifted you are—you are responsible for how you use the gifts God has given you.

[Your gift is God's gift to you. What you do with that gift is your gift back to God.] There are so many gifted people who attend church that just sit there not contributing to anything. Get in the game. Get in the fight. Start serving.

The only two swords that were in Israel were tucked away safely, hidden in a tent. Now that's depressing. David wasn't planning on leading from the tent. He was going to lead from the battlefield. God always leads us to the battlefields.

King Saul must have not even seen much potential in David because he tried to dress him in his armor.

Of course that wouldn't have worked. Saul was much bigger than David. David was a young man and had a smaller build. Saul was a tall man that stood above the crowds. David would have looked like me trying to preach like T. D. Jakes—ridiculous. If David was going to win this battle, he had to be himself.

[Goliath had more weapons than Israel had ever seen before. David chose five stones. David used what was available to him. You don't need a building, a microphone, or a social media account to impact your city. You just need to use what's in your hand to fulfill what's in your heart.]

What do you have in your hand *right now*? Start with that.

You can spend so much time complaining about what you don't have and miss out on what you do have.

David could have used any excuse he wanted to get out of this fight. He could have waited until they had the perfect swords, perfect strategy, and perfect chariots to make the jump.

But he had that ride-or-die mentality. We all know the story. If you don't, you can read the whole story in 1 Samuel 17. David didn't look like much and his enemy underestimated him. *Everyone* underestimated him. He was the little guy. I can imagine everyone's surprise when David took the fight to Goliath and ran toward him.

If you want to know what servanthood really looks like, here it is:

David said to the Philistine, "You come against me with sword and spear and javelin, but I come against you in the name of the Lord Almighty, the God of the armies of Israel, whom you have defied. This day the Lord will deliver you into my hands, and I'll strike you down and cut off your head. This very day I will give the carcasses of the Philistine army to the birds and the wild animals, and the whole world will know that there is a God in Israel. All those gathered here will know that it is not by sword or spear that the Lord saves; for the battle is the Lord's, and he will give all of you into our hands." As the Philistine moved closer to attack him, David ran quickly toward the battle line to meet him.

(1 Samuel 17:45–48)

David was willing to give his life for a cause greater than his own. Craig Groeshel once said, "People will work for a 'what' but they will give their lives for a 'why.'" He nailed it.

It was the "why" behind David's passion to take action. This was bigger than turf wars. It was bigger than him trying to make a name for himself and become famous. This was a personal injustice he was seeing that couldn't go unanswered.

David was a man I would follow in a heartbeat. His type of spirit is what I want surrounding me. I want people who are willing to put it all on the line and run toward the needs in our world. I want people willing to embrace a vision for how they can use their gifts in our church so together we can make a big difference in our city. I want to serve alongside people who are willing to put their reputations on the line and live with a sense of urgency that we will give everything we have to see change happen in our world.

We are better together. And wouldn't you know that the same people who were scared in their tents were so inspired by David's passion that when they saw Goliath fall, those same people were full of faith to chase after their enemies and kill them all. What changed?

Bigger weapons? More people? More conferences? Longer prayer meetings? Longer worship sets?

Nope. It was because one person was willing to serve. David was committed to breaking the mold.

People do what people see.

I would love to have seen the look on David's brothers' faces when they saw him slay the giant. I would love to know what was going through their head when that young man was standing there with the head of the giant.

That was the first time that King Saul took notice of David and wanted to know who this man was. That was the moment he began to realize there was something different about this kid.

The children of Israel won the battle and pursued the Philistines in front of them because of one man's obedience to serve.

There's not a person in all of history who was more obedient than Jesus. Jesus left heaven, where there was no shortage of worship, to come down to us so we would have the opportunity to be awakened to the story of God. He did this for the Father's glory. Jesus valued the Father so much that He was willing to fight for us to restore us back to Himself. If Jesus served with that type of commitment, it should be the most normal thing imaginable for followers of Jesus to dedicate their entire lives to that type of servanthood for others.

The Bible says we are the light of the world:

> In the same way, let your light shine before men that they may see your good deeds and glorify your Father in heaven.
>
> (Matthew 5:16)

We are not just lights in the world. We are illuminators of the great plan of God in the world—so much so that people would become worshipers of Him because of our light. That requires us to get into the dark places and get our hands messy.

Let me tell you something about VIVE Culture. We are in the world and we're really happy about that. We are not of the world but yes we are in the world.

It's our pleasure to be able to follow after Jesus and serve with everything we have been given.

Steven Furtick once said, "The most extraordinary moves of God begin with the most ordinary acts of obedience." Don't take for granted the power of ordinary obedience. Don't take for granted your contribution and your faithful obedience. When you plant and serve in God's house with the gifts you've been given with every fiber of your being, you join with the heartbeat of God to impact your city.

You will soon discover that the more you are around those types of spirits, the more you will see that it becomes such a privilege to serve. Whatever God has entrusted you with, do it with all your heart. Nothing is insignificant when done for the most significant purpose on earth, which is to advance the gospel to every people group in our world.

Stay faithful. Parents, keep serving your kids. Students, keep serving your peers. Don't stop. Pastors and leaders, keep serving your city.

What defines us, who we are, and what we are called to every second of every day is sustained by, empowered by, and held together by our relationship with God and His purpose for our existence. When you have that type of confidence, serving becomes easier.

Jesus is committed to growing the church for reaching, building, and helping people and finishing that work in and through us. He's committed to sending us to the darkest places of the world.

Let's do this together. Let's be all in! We need to stop asking God to bless our plans and start aligning our hearts with His plans that He has promised in His Word to bless. If we do that, I believe He'll move greatly on our behalf.

Louie Giglio, one of my favorite communicators and lead pastor of Passion City Church, said something once that I will never forget:

To be a force for good, the Church must rise up to take its place in the world. As the people of God, our calling comes with a gigantic opportunity to be God's representatives to spread His fame—not just within the walls of the church, but everywhere we go. That's our beautiful role in the unending and life-giving story of God. Humanity is waiting and God is counting on us to shine, serve, and love His people for the salvation and common good of all. We are the light of the world, door holders for His glory, and called to be restorers of the city. The

Potential and Power of the People of God for the Greater Good of the Whole Wide World.

That's so powerful. We want to show our city that Jesus is the best thing that has ever happened to us . . . there's not even a close second. He is everything to us and is worthy of everything. It is not a "have to" thing. To us, it's a "that we may" thing.

Together we are a force for good.

I'm so grateful to my former pastor for putting his arm around me and releasing me to be myself before I even believed in myself. I think the best leaders release people to lead before they are even ready. If I'm being completely honest, I've never been ready for any new season God asked us to step into.

Certain leaders in my life released me to lead before I was ready or before I even believed in myself. And I'm so grateful that they did.

Now, I not only lead our team like it's a family, but I desire for our church to feel like a home. Church isn't an organization you belong to but a family that you join. I want VIVE to act like a home, look like a home, and feel like a home.

I love that I get to do life with my team. It's so much fun. Together, we are passionate about our assignment that moves us outside the walls of our church and into the cracks and corners of our communities to bring real life change to those who need it most.

I pray the common thread of all our streams, ministries, and all our different walks of life is a tribe that embraces a spirit of honor, humility, and servanthood.

My hope is that people will look at us and say, "I don't know what it is about them but they just serve with an uncommon joy and have some of the kindest hearts I've ever known. They love unconditionally with no strings attached and give so generously that there is no other way to describe them other than Christians."

This is the type of church we are always striving to become!

3

if not us . . . then who?

I love the Ultimate Fighting Championship, or the UFC. There's something electrifying about two people in a cage trying to impose their will on one another. The UFC isn't just a guy sport. If you have ever watched it, the women's fights are just as exciting. The female fighters are just as skilled as the male fighters. They are incredible athletes. It's an amazing sport . . . which is why I was so excited when the movie *Warrior* came out in 2011. It was a rebranded version of Rocky.

Who didn't love Rocky growing up? I'm Italian and grew up in an Italian home. I don't know any Italian man who didn't think he was the Italian Stallion.

If you didn't get a lump in your throat during Rocky IV when Rocky took out Iron Man Drago and shouted, "Adrian!" you potentially could be dead inside.

The movie Warrior had that type of emotional impact. It is a powerful story of two brothers who ended up in two different places in life because one brother chose to hold on to bitterness and hate while the other chose to do something great with his life despite what he had walked through. The first time Alicia and I watched it I looked over at her toward the end and she was balling.

There I was watching a man's movie and my wife was next to me crying. What was happening? I'll admit, at the end when the older brother held his younger brother who hated him and said, "It's okay Tommy. It's okay. I love you," as he was submitting him, there was a huge lump in my throat that I was trying to get control over.

All I can say is my allergies were kicking in really strong during that moment in the movie. To me, the movie *Warrior* isn't really about the UFC. It's a story of grace.

Grace is a powerful thing, isn't it? Grace is one of those things that, even if you've grown up in church, can seem confusing. We sing songs about grace, read about it, and hear messages about it, but many times we don't really get it.

It's sort of like when you receive an awkward present from someone that you don't know what to do with. Have you ever been there? It's the type of present you only pull out when you know that person is coming over. Otherwise you hide it away in the basement.

I was the first one on my side of the family that had a baby.

Overnight, my daughter Kaitlyn became the center of my parents and grandparents' world. When my grandparents would come over to our house, you would have thought no one else existed in the world. I loved it.

I remember when Kaitlyn was two years old my mom decided that what we needed in our home was a five-foot-tall porcelain doll with the biggest eyes I had ever seen in my life. This doll was twice the size of Kaitlyn at the time.

I started laughing when my mom brought it out. I mean seriously. What are we supposed to do with a five-foot-tall porcelain doll?

The first night we had it in Kaitlyn's room she woke up screaming because it scared her. Can you blame her? That was the last night that doll was inside our home. It only came out when my mom would visit. After that it went back in the garage.

Grace can feel a lot like that to many people. We only bring it out when we are around other churched people, but otherwise it kind of goes back in the garage. What do we do with it? How does it really play out in our everyday lives? That's a great question to ask. Nothing has impacted my perspective of grace and loving people who are hard to love like becoming a parent. Dads, as tough as we try to be, there's something about our kids that gets inside our hearts. They don't even need to say a word. Just one look can break you down.

My daughter London, who I talked about in the last chapter, has a number of great qualities about her. She is strong, loyal, determined, and full of courage. I can see her leading her own company someday. However, a spirit of grace is a quality we are still trying to develop in her. On one particular day it seemed like we were doing a lot of character coaching with London because of her attitude. She would make a bad decision, we would correct it, and we would move on. But then, ten minutes later, she would make another bad decision. We would correct it, and move on. It was just one of those days. At the same time my son, Riley, who was seven years old at the time, also made a bad decision and wasn't treating his sisters the way a man should be treating ladies. I only know this because I got word of it from London.

I'm hard on my sons in a few areas and one area is the way they treat their mom and sisters because that's shaping them for how they will be as a husband and dad someday. Apparently Riley deeply offended London by his actions. So she stomped up the stairs and interrupted me watching my Blackhawks taking on the Ducks.

It wasn't the most convenient time to have a heart-to heart. However, she had that look in her eyes. London has the ability to transform her deep browns that lets you know she's about to unload the wrath of God on you. When she gets mad she looks like a little cute, slightly possessed Ewok on Star Wars.

London was fed up. She was all business. I could tell this was one of those parenting moments that couldn't wait until the second intermission. I muted the TV and she began to spill this amazing, dramatized, very detailed story about how Riley mistreated her. She was all worked up.

I heard her side of the story and said, "That must have felt awful. I'm sorry he hurt your heart. What would you like me to do?"

I thought she was going to say that she needed a hug, or that maybe an ice cream cone would fix it. I should have been more attentive, but it was a really close game.

"What is so bad that can't be cured with an ice cream cone?" I thought to myself.

London wasn't budging.

London looked at me with that crinkled up face and said "Dad, go make him pay. Let's get him."

Easy wonder woman. This girl is crazy.

She grabbed my hand and pulled me up. Now I'm committed. So I called Riley up to my room to see if he actually did what London said because if you have any experience in raising kids, you know that there are always two sides to every story—and the person crying isn't always the victim.

You have to understand that my son Riley is a dream to parent. He is an amazing kid. He is so kindhearted, patient and one of the most flexible boys you will ever meet. He is always finding ways to take care of people. For being around girls all the time, he is so patient it is unbelievable. He's just the coolest kid. I can't say enough about how much I respect him.

As much as I love him, he knows he's been in deep trouble over the years for how he has treated and responded to his mom and sisters. I believe I'm raising a man to honor and respect women. So no matter how mad he may feel, he needs to take responsibility for how he responds.

So you could imagine how hard it was for me to believe that London was telling the whole story.

So I kept it light at first and said, "Son, a case has been brought before me and if it's true, you are in trouble."

Of course London was standing right there by me with her arms folded, starring at Riley as if to say, "Oooo you are going to get it. Daddy, *get him!*"

I said to him, "Be honest son. Were you disrespectful to you sister?"

"Yes I was," Riley said.

My tone of voice changed and instantly it became a serious moment.

"So after you said that, did you then take it a step further and treat her this way—even after you disrespected her?" I replied.

"You know what Dad, yes I did," he said in a softer voice.

Now I was fired up. That was my baby girl he was disrespecting. It was time to bring down the hammer and flex the daddy muscles.

So I went on to say, "Do you have anything to say for yourself before I come down on you with the punishment? What you did was absolutely unacceptable and it's time to pay for the decisions you made."

Obviously London was sitting there with a grin thinking, "Oooo . . . you are going to get it. You go daddy. I'm so proud of you. Get him."

Now when I talk to my son and get firm with him, he gets this raspy voice and his lip quivers. However, my son is becoming a man and he's trying to be strong with me. He stood there for a moment—but I wasn't expecting what would come out of his mouth next.

With his head down Riley said in a raspy voice, "Dad, just know before you say anything and decide what to do, I want you to know this . . . I really love you. I own it. I messed up. I'm so sorry and I'll try to be better."

I became like a melted ice cream cone on a hot summer day. Now I was biting my lip trying not to cry in front of my son. I lost it.

I grabbed Riley and pulled him up into my arms and said, "I'm so proud of you. Come here and give me a hug. That's what being a man is all about. Of course you are forgiven son. Do you want to come and watch the game with me and have some popcorn?"

I wish you could have seen the look on London's face.

"That's it! Dad I said *get* him!" London shouted with her crinkled up face.

I was like, "Honey, shhh! Go away . . . we are having a man moment here."

The look on London's face when I went from judge to forgiver was priceless. London wanted tears. She wanted Riley to pay. It's funny, though, how she forgot all the times during that day where I could have made *her* pay, but chose to extend grace instead.

Grace is a funny thing. It can seem so unfair until we are in need of it ourselves.

There is something about grace and what it does for us when we deserve something but get grace instead that is life changing. A little bit of grace makes room for a whole lot of truth.

[I have found that such a powerful way to serve others around us is by extending grace to them.] In fact, the more I keep my ears open to what people are walking through and the more I see how dark our world is becoming, the more I see how much more grace we need in our world today. We need so much more grace in our words, in our posts, and our social media conversations. We need more grace in our tone of voice regarding our leaders and influencers.

I grew up in a day in age where the Church was all about judgment. Christians who wanted everyone else to pay for their sin surrounded me.

As a kid, I would hear Christians say things like, "God, thank you that we aren't like them."

I would hear messages that said, "We're just going to hold on until Jesus comes back." I'm sure I'm not alone, but growing up, some of the meanest, unforgiving people I knew were Christians.

I grew up in a very traditional church. When you hear "traditional church," you may think of pews and an organ—but that wasn't our church. Our church simply had a more traditional approach in how it viewed its role in the community. I think there is such beauty in diversity in the body of Christ. Not every church is called to be Hillsong, Elevation, or North Point Church.

There are so many different types of people in our world and we need different types of churches to reach them all. The people in my church growing up were really kind and those in leadership loved God with all their hearts. They loved our family and we loved them. There were some senior citizens in that church who taught me what it really meant to have a prayer life. They had such sweet spirits.

As kind as those people were, that church was designed for a traditional church attendee.

I remember I brought my friend one time that was not churched at all. He felt so unwelcome and received so many comments about how he dressed and the hat he wore that he never wanted to go back.

[I didn't know how to process it all as a young man but I kept telling myself, as I got older, "Something isn't right. What I'm reading in the Bible isn't exactly lining up with what I'm seeing in the Church as a whole. Why are we surprised that people in the world act like they do? They don't have Jesus. Shouldn't the Church constantly be finding new ways to connect with the culture we are now living in, not the culture that existed twenty years ago?"

The local church should be the most loving, welcoming place for people to feel like they belong. The local church should be an extension of heaven on earth where we find a permanent home. It should have such a magnetic atmosphere that when people walk in it's the best part of their week. We should be finding new ways to keep reaching people in our culture in a way they can understand. Why do people have to go away from the church to see creativity, passion, and authenticity?]

[I understand no church is perfect.]

I love the people of that church. I served as the drummer for years as a young teenager every weekend, and they continue to do a great job caring for the people they are called to pastor. They are so faithful to serve and love the people of their community. That pastor I grew up with is still a friend to our family.

[As I look back, it wasn't about the church I grew up in. It was about what Jesus was doing in my heart.] I wish I responded differently. But of course, as a young teenager, I thought I knew everything.

So instead of taking my questions to Jesus, and talking it through with people who were spiritually mature to help me process what I was feeling, I made the mistake of walking away from it all. That decision took me down a very dark, lonely, and dangerous road.

Thank God for grace and for the prayers of family members that didn't give up on me.

When I fully gave my life to Jesus when I was sixteen years old a passion ignited in me that has yet to go out. [I was convinced that if people understood how loving, amazing, and incredible the love of Jesus really is, it would change everything for them.]

I envisioned a church being so relational, so alive, and so welcoming that people who are far from God will fall in love with Him because of the Spirit in His people. I pictured a church that was so creative we could engage our culture in a way they could relate to.

It was an awakening moment for me as a teenager. The closer I grew to Jesus and studied His footsteps, the greater the stirring in my heart was to fight for grace for people.

To fight for people's justice.

To believe that the best is still to come for every person's story, even if they weren't living up to their fullest potential . . . yet.

One of the most life-transforming things we can do to serve our world is to show grace to people.

I'll admit I don't know all the ins-and-outs of what grace is. I'm still learning what it means. However, I can speak from my own story and tell you that I was a messed-up person before I met Jesus.

I grew up in a Christian home and started playing drums in our traditional church when I was ten years old. I attended church every Sunday morning and every Sunday night for years. Even then, I didn't really have a real relationship with Jesus for myself. I was going through the motions but nothing really attracted me to His way of living.

It was like reading all about the Grand Canyon and seeing pictures—which is great—but it wasn't until I experienced it for myself that everything changed.

[I can't do anything halfway. I am loyal to a fault. So, I couldn't follow Jesus halfway. Not surprisingly, when I made the decision to totally give up on the idea of Jesus for myself, I became a teenager full of hate, bitterness, and resentment. That's the problem with sin.

It promises a more fulfilled life away from Jesus and costs more than you can possibly imagine.]

God's grace is so amazing to me. I'm so thankful that during those years when I was running that all of heaven was chasing me down. And it wasn't a song that saved me. It wasn't attending an event. It was a longer message that captured my heart. It was grace through Jesus. Despite the challenges I was walking through, I had a circle of people who believed in me, stood by me, and were in the fight of my life with me.

Giving people a little bit of grace goes a long way.

I finally had a defining moment in the middle of a baseball field one night that would change the course of my life. His grace astounded me when I realized He still wanted me despite what I had become. I finally realized that at the heart of it all we were made for a relationship with the Creator of the universe.

Grace isn't just what Jesus has done for us. It's who He is. He is Grace.

The more you take time to listen to people's stories, the more you realize that every person is the way they are because of their experiences. What would our world look like if instead of looking at people like my daughter London did and saying "Ooooh! You are going to get it. Jesus get them!" we stood by people and served them even if they haven't arrived yet? What if we loved people through the junk they are walking through? It's possible to fully love people and serve them even if they believe the complete opposite of what you believe.

There's not one person on this planet that is a finished product yet.

Jesus believed people were worth fighting for.

Jennie Allen, author of the book *Nothing to Prove* said, "Wisely invest in only two things that won't die: God and people. You want to know the answer to cynicism? Start building things. Then there's no energy left to tear things down."

Isn't that truth? It's so much easier to have a critical spirit when you aren't serving. When you are invested in other people, it's so much easier to extend grace. When you begin to serve your city, you start seeing through a whole different set of lenses.

When you start investing your life in building people up . . . it feels criminal to tear someone down. It's not breaking news to anyone that there isn't a whole lot of grace left in our world—especially with social media taking over where everyone is fascinated by headlines, even if they don't understand the story. We live in a vicious world ready to take you out the moment you show signs of weakness.

There are a whole lot of Christian reactions but not a whole lot of graceful responses today.

[Can you stand alongside someone for the long haul, even if they haven't arrived? Can you still love and serve people, even if they aren't ready to hear truth? Can you extend grace to someone, even if they don't believe anything you stand for?

Because if not us . . . then who?]

A SIMPLIFIED WAY OF LIVING

One of the main reasons I love studying the life of Jesus is because he bypasses all the nonsense and gets to the bottom line.

I'm a bottom-line person. Have you ever met a person that takes seven years to get to the point of the story? It took them so long to get to the point that by the time they got there you forgot half the details to what they were even talking about. I'm one of those people. If a person takes too long to get to the point, I start thinking of other things while they are telling their story. I feel so bad about it.

For example, you know by now that I'm a Cliffs Notes person. When I call my mom to check in to see how she and my dad are feeling, we talk for ten minutes and then we hang up. Right when I hang up the phone my wife will ask me about the conversation. So I'll sum it up in 140 characters.

If you know my wife, that's not good enough. She'll ask, "Then what happened?"

I'll reply, "I don't know."

"Well what did that person say when they heard that?" she'll continue.

"I'm not sure."

Alicia will continue and say, "Well what's going to happen next?"

"I'm not sure; I didn't ask."

Alicia will not let it go and will say, "Well, how did it make them feel when they found out?"

I love my wife because she wants to know details. Alicia is a person who brings so much joy and life to everyone she meets. I'm sure that knowing more details makes the sky bluer and the grass greener.

I am a bottom-line personality. I figure if people want me to know about anything, they will tell me.

Jesus is a bottom-line leader. I love that about Him. It's easy to spend so much time working, fighting, and investing in something that isn't close to God's heart. So Jesus makes it easy. He sums it up.

✗ [Let me tell you why you are here. You're here to be salt-seasoning that brings out the God-flavors of this earth. If you lose your saltiness, how will people taste godliness? You've lost your usefulness and will end up in the garbage. Here's another way to put it:

You're here to be light, bringing out the God-colors in the world. God is not a secret to be kept.

We're going public with this, as public as a city on a hill. If I make you light-bearers, you don't think I'm going to hide you under a bucket, do you? I'm putting you on a light stand. Now that I've put you there on a hilltop, on a light stand—shine! Keep open house; be generous with your lives. By opening up to others, you'll prompt people to open up with God, this generous Father in heaven.] ✗

(Matthew 5:13–16 MSG)

I love this because Jesus exposes two different ways we are called to serve in this world.

The first one is salt.

Salt is only effective if it comes in contact with something. Salt doesn't change anything in the pantry. This is going to mess some of us up because some of us love to be pantry Christians.

As long as no one gets hurt, as long as we stay out of trouble, I'm good.

I think it's great that we pray for people, but there comes a time when you have to get off your knees and get in the ring with people and fight alongside them. You have to get outside your circles and get out into the community.

I love popcorn. Our family loves to make popcorn on the stove. When we need to make it quick, we have a certain microwave brand that we like to make. However, popcorn doesn't really hit the spot until just the right amount of salt is on it. Popcorn by itself is dry and bland, but when you put the right amount of butter and salt on it, it's a taste of heaven.

[In Jesus' day, salt was a valued commodity. Roman soldiers were sometimes paid with salt, giving rise to the phrase "worth his salt." Salt was valuable because it would preserve meat from decay making it last longer. Christians are like salt because they have a preserving influence in the cities in which we live in.]

That's right. Christians should be influential in our world. I can't imagine what our world would look like without Christian leaders in our schools, court systems, or in our military.

In addition, salt adds flavor.

You're here to be salt-seasoning that brings out the God-flavors of this earth.

I don't know about you, but I'm tired of seeing and listening to grumpy, complaining, negative, sarcastic Christians. I'm tired of reading negative posts on social media.

I'm so tired of hearing criticism all the time of our leaders, friends, kids, and so on. We shouldn't be the grumpy, complaining, critical ones where no one wants to be around us. We are supposed to be different. Our tone of voice should be bringing out the God-flavors in this world, stirring hearts to want to know Him more. It should be refreshing when people are around Jesus followers. Our tone of voice should be filled with grace.

I heard it once said that people should "leave feeling better about themselves, not you" when they cross our path.

I love that.

[We can love and serve people well even if people don't vote like us, believe like us, or parent like us.]

If the salt loses its flavor it's good for nothing. I believe we can be a church that is full of grace for people. I believe we can lead a movement where we speak life over people and can be a refreshing voice in society.

I feel a deep passion to champion people because someone did that for me and, I would assume you could say someone did that for you, too. However, only when it comes in contact with something and is used at the right time in the right way does salt bring out God-flavors.

My daughter, Makayla, loves salt too much, in fact. She has to have her own bowl because she takes the saltshaker and dumps the entire thing on the popcorn. Her popcorn is so bitter!

Makayla can take a bowl of popcorn, ready to be enjoyed, and ruin it. How? It's too much. It's really not about the salt. It's about the popcorn. But too often people are so self-consumed and focused on the wrong issues and give the wrong responses that it's a turn off. It's too much.

[I have found that a lot of times people aren't turned off to Jesus as much as the person delivering the message.]

[We are called to be salt to bring out the God-flavors in this world, but that means you have to engage with culture the right way. You have to run toward the marginalized the right way. You have to be in the community the right way. When we don't serve with the right spirit, it's like that bitter-tasting popcorn that leaves you feeling sick.]

The second aspect Jesus called us to be is light:

[Now that I've put you there on a hilltop, on a light stand—shine! By opening up to others, you'll prompt people to open up with God, this generous Father in heaven.]

(Matthew 5:16 MSG)

Light is meant to spread out and expose, which means there is a time to expose, stand up, and lead—but it's on the platform and with the tone of voice of grace to lead people to Jesus. Jesus never challenges us to become salt and light. He says we *are* salt and light.

Jesus had this amazing ability to look through the lenses of grace and see a person not for who they were but who they would become. We see this in Jesus' life when He called one of His future disciples.

After this, Jesus went out and saw a tax collector by the name of Levi sitting at his tax booth. "Follow me," Jesus said to him.

(Luke 5:27)

Tax collectors in those days were despised by their own culture. They worked for the Roman government but grew rich off fellow Jews by collecting excess money to enrich their personal lives. The religious people despised them—so much so that they believed even spending time with tax collectors would ruin their reputation.

No one went out of their way to serve tax collectors. No one would ever be caught dead sharing life with them. Yet Jesus locked eyes with Levi and extended this invitation to him: follow me.

Levi's response is perfect.

And Levi got up, left everything and followed him.

(Luke 5:28)

Now, notice that Jesus didn't take him through the ten perfect ways to be a follower of Jesus. He didn't go through a list of everything Levi was doing wrong. He didn't look at Levi with disgust. Jesus extended the invitation, and Levi followed. Levi's journey with Jesus started with followship before he was called to leadership. Notice what Jesus did next. It's brilliant:

Then Levi held a great banquet for Jesus at his house, and a large crowd of tax collectors and others were eating with them. But the Pharisees and the teachers of the law who belonged to their sect complained to his disciples, "Why do you eat and drink with tax collectors and sinners?" Jesus answered them, "It is not the healthy who need a doctor, but the sick. I have not come to call the righteous, but sinners to repentance."

(Luke 5:29–32)

Jesus went straight for the heart on this one. Jesus was unraveling everything these religious people stood for. They didn't want to associate with sinners. The Pharisees were extremely racist. They didn't want to engage with anyone outside of their race. They certainly didn't see through eyes of grace. The religious leaders thought that serving tax collectors was beneath them. They thought their reputations would be ruined if they ever sat with a sinner.

Jesus was saying, "That is the whole reason why I came!"

Jesus is basically saying, "If not us . . . then who?"

Jesus was sitting in the home of those sinners showing us today that the way to a person's heart isn't through religion; it is through relationship.

By opening up to others Jesus allowed Levi—known to fellow Jews by his Hebrew name, Matthew—to see there was more to life than he was living for. And it all started with grace.

Jesus didn't see a Levi. He saw a Matthew. He didn't see a tax collector. He saw a future follower of Jesus. Too often we see people for where they are not where they should be.

I don't know how to explain it perfectly, but there's something about a person's level of grace that they extend to others when they have actually been through some stuff. When you have walked through heartache and suffering, for example, it changes the amount of grace you show others. When you are a parent and are in the fight every day, it changes how critical you are of other parents. When you have experienced betrayal and injustice, it changes the way you look at injustice.

[The level of grace a person shows others is directly related to their understanding of grace for themselves.]

GRACE GROWS THROUGH OUR EXPERIENCES

When my family first moved out to Kansas City, it was such a hard season for all of us. We felt called to leave California during a time when the entire market was crashing in America. It seemed like everyone was foreclosing on their homes and was out of work. We felt called to step out to help a church plant in Colorado when our lead pastor at the time took a different position in Southern California.

From the first day we moved to Colorado, we soon discovered the church we thought we interviewed for was in real trouble. The first day we moved into town several people on the team quit and as time went on it was clear this church wasn't going to make it. The lead pastor was a great guy and we loved his family, but he was just in the wrong role. Now he is absolutely crushing in his new role impacting people on the streets and in prisons.

Looking back now, however, we would have asked vastly different questions than the ones we did when we were younger. To make a long story short, the church was on life support and we had to make a change. So we moved to Kansas City.

We have always loved Kansas City. Alicia and I always talked about the potential of one day raising our kids here. It's an amazing city to raise a family in. I believe Kansas City is one of the best-kept secrets from most of America. It's no surprise that it's one of the fastest growing cities in America. Alicia has nine other brothers and sisters and they were all born and raised in Kansas City. It's her hometown.

About a week after we officially moved to Kansas City, I was driving around downtown and I looked at her and said, "What if we planted a church here?"

We had just come from a rough portable church experience so it was no surprise that Alicia wasn't open to it at the time. What we thought was going to be a smooth transition to KC ended up becoming a very lonely season for us.

We made the move during the time when the market crashed, everyone was losing their jobs, and no churches were hiring anywhere. I had all this church experience and everywhere I looked churches were making cuts. So getting a ministry job became almost impossible. To make matters worse, I didn't know one person in Kansas City. I didn't have one friend and I didn't know anyone that I could just hang out with. My entire network and life was back in California.

We had just had our third baby and thankfully my in-laws were so gracious and took in our family of five and allowed us to live with them while we waited for God to open a door.

What we thought would be a couple of months turned into a year. They were amazing about it, though.

We had to sell what we couldn't take with us and put everything else we owned in storage and basically lived out of our closest for the entire year. I don't think anyone really knew how lonely I was. It was the closest I ever was to going into full-out depression. I was so miserable and I didn't have anyone to talk to and share what I was really experiencing. I battled the spirit of depression every day.

Everyone had friendships and family in Kansas City. I didn't have one person I really knew or could talk to.

Of course, I had two toddlers who were in heaven being around family and my first baby boy who was stuck to his momma's hip. So they loved it. My wife had her family and was in the home she grew up in.

I tried to stay positive and strong for Alicia and the kids when they were around by burying everything I felt inside. But there was no question; I was on the brink of being depressed.

Every single day I wanted to load up a U-Haul and move back to California and never look back again.

Inside, my spirit was growing angrier and angrier, until one evening when Alicia and I were talking out on her parent's deck. It was one of those nights in Kansas City that you live for. It was a gorgeous night. As she was talking about things she and her sisters were laughing about that day, and how much fun the kids had with their cousins, I started to realize that I needed a heart adjustment. I told myself as I was going to bed that night that if I was going to go through this season, I might as well learn what God was trying to teach me from it.

Not all days were perfect, but thankfully, my father-in-law was kind enough to hire me to work for his construction company temporarily while we did ministry here and there throughout the community. On top of that, I also got a job at Chili's as a server during the evening shifts for extra income.

My poor father-in-law. He was a successful businessman who owned his own construction company and could build and fix anything. If you need anything fixed or built, I have no doubt my father-in-law can do it. Not only can he build things, he can work on cars, too. How cool is that?

My father-in-law kept building on to the house Alicia grew up in. I can't even build a Lego house without it falling apart. It's pathetic. I have a tough time playing the game Jenga. One time when my son Riley was five years old he asked me to help him build wooden box in our garage out of four pieces of wood. I have no idea why I couldn't take four pieces of wood that were the exact same size and make a square box.

It's seriously a gift how bad I am at building things. Afterward Riley said with a confused look on his face, "I wonder if we can call Pops to see if he can fix this."

I'm okay with it. I'm not a handy man at all. You would think that God would take it easy on me and give me a little talent in that area but I just don't have that mind to work construction. Knowing that, I should have been fired from his construction company. Only God knows how much money I cost him for him to redo things.

Even though I wasn't any good at it, I actually really enjoyed working for him. He was a great boss. Everyone loved working for him. And surprisingly, I really loved working at Chili's as well. Well, the actual job was awful but the people were amazing. By the grace of God, my family became friends with the whole team at Chili's. I was surrounded by homosexuals, atheists, party-loving people, and people who were sleeping around—and in the middle of it all, there was me, a pastor.

I loved them.

I remember one night we were wrapping up silverware in the back and I was talking to this guy and a girl who both were both in separate homosexual relationships and we were having the best time laughing about life. I remember my friend—we'll call him Johnny just to keep his name private—said to me, "I have never met a Christian I actually liked before. You don't seem to be grossed out by us. You are actually easy to talk to."

I felt so hurt that he experienced that from people. I don't know how people couldn't like being around these two individuals. Why would I be grossed out? They were amazing people. They were so kind, fun, smart, and had incredible potential inside of them. The story didn't end with some amazing moment that led them to Jesus. I had the opportunity to share my story of grace and why I love Jesus. I don't know where they are right now. Who knows if that one conversation one day leads them to find Jesus through someone else. I pray it does.

Going through that season taught me more about caring for people and loving people who are walking through difficult seasons themselves than anything I had ever experienced.

When you walk through pain and suffering, it's so much easier for you to extend grace to others.

> Do you see this woman? I came to your home; you provided no water for my feet, but she rained tears on my feet and dried them with her hair. You gave me no greeting, but from the time I arrived she hasn't quit kissing my feet. You provided nothing for freshening up, but she has soothed my feet with perfume. Impressive, isn't it? She was for-given many, many sins, and so she is very, very grateful. If the forgive-ness is minimal, the gratitude is minimal.
>
> (Luke 7:44–47 MSG)

Personally experiencing the grace and mercy of Jesus changes the way you love and look at other people. It changes what you live for. It changes how you are salt and light to the world around you.

Some of the most passionate worshipers, givers, and servers are those who have experienced what it's like to be away from Jesus and are filled with so much gratitude because of the grace He's shown us. It's not hard for me as the father of my kids to extend grace because there's a deep rela-tionship. I love them. I don't expect my two-year-old son, Jude, to act like a thirty-seven-year-old man. There's a process they go through.

Yes, it's exhausting. It's challenging. But that's what love and grace is all about. So many times we give up on people because we expect them to be three decades into their journey with Jesus when they are just starting out. Why do we get disgusted with the world? They are supposed to be like that. They don't have the love of Jesus. Where would we be if not for grace? A little bit of grace opens up room for a whole lot of truth.

When you really love people, it's easier to extend grace to them.

Too often we forget how much we needed grace and are in need of grace daily and then we start acting like my five-year-old London and say, "Ooo, you're gonna get it." I'm so glad Jesus didn't do that to us when He was hanging on the cross. Instead of saying, "God, get them!" He was a perfect picture of grace and said, "Forgive them, Father, for they don't know what they are doing."

That's grace.

GRACE IN MOTION

When we were the family pastors in California, there was a student who was full of anger when we first met him. He had zero emotion, and he wouldn't talk to me. If I asked him a question, he wouldn't answer me.

This young man was a killer basketball player on the Varsity team but he always wore raggedy shoes with holes in them. Even though he acted like he hated me, he always showed up with his friends. We'd play ball together on the court with the other guys and he wouldn't say one word to me. Come to find out his whole family moved from LA and they were deeply involved in the gang life out there.

Six family members lived in a single hotel room right next to our church with no food, and he didn't have money to pay for new shoes. His mother was dying of cancer and his brother, who was two years older, was dealing drugs. I caught where they were staying and went to bring him the new Jordan sneakers I bought him for his new season coming up.

I took the shoes over to him and when he answered the door you could tell he was a little annoyed that I found him there. The whole room smelled like weed. He didn't say anything to me. I told him that I was proud of him, I was excited to watch him play, and I simply wanted to bless him with these shoes.

He looked at me and said thanks and went back inside. His mother ended up passing away and a few months later and a rival gang killed his brother on the streets. Over time this young man gave his heart to the Lord and never missed a Wednesday.

Not one. Once the walls were broken down, he ended up being one of the kindest students ever. Over time, we were able to hang out, hoop, and laugh together because I had built trust. He was the first person to ever graduate from high school in his family and he eventually graduated college. [He had to live with several different people to make it but a little bit a grace made room for a whole lot of truth. He became a "somebody" because a lot of people believed in him.]

Compassion isn't truly compassion until you cross the street and do something.

It's easy to see people with a lot of money, who have huge houses, and have impressive titles, and make assumptions about them. But whether someone is on the streets or lives in luxury, we all have the same holes in our hearts that can only be filled by Jesus. Understand me when I say that a time will come when you have to tell the life-changing truth of who God is and what He stands for. But when that time comes you'll have the grace platform to stand on. I'm not saying put your head in the sand and just agree with everything people are doing that is destroying their life. [However, our tone of voice should always be from a place of grace where they feel like you are for them not against them.]

It's not about trying to impress people with how smart you are. It's about making an eternal difference in people's lives. It's about making a difference in people not simply trying to make a point.

God made him who had no sin to be sin for us, so that in him we might become the righteousness of God.

(2 Corinthians 5:21)

Here's the bottom line.

Grace paid the bill. When you know grace paid the bill you can begin to step out and invest in people that seem like they are a lost cause because the same grace that called you is the same grace that's going to cover you.

You can step out and take chances on people. You can be close friends with people even if they stand on the opposite political spectrum than you. You can let people lead things even if they aren't all put together yet because of what you see in them because it isn't about you or your reputation. It's about drawing out what God sees in them. A life of servanthood is a life that gives people an opportunity to flourish in their calling.

If you want to be a world-changer, start serving people. Start calling out the Matthew in your student. Start calling the Matthew out in your marriage. Start calling out the Matthew in your relationships. Start calling out the Matthew in your city.

Your spouse may not be where they need to be yet, but you are going to keep fighting for them. Your teen may not be where they need to be, but you are going to keep building that relationship with them and speaking life into them. Your work environment may feel toxic at times but you are going to choose to bring life to that place because of who lives inside of you.

Because if not us . . . then who?

Life's too short and eternity is too long to be playing games.

So no, we won't settle down about injustice and be quiet because it's not a political issue, it's a Jesus issue. We're not going to settle down and be silent about racism because racism isn't a skin issue, it's a sin issue. We aren't going to ignore it like it isn't happening but instead we are going to stand up—because if not us . . . then who?

Grace is more of a heart posture than a position. When you are aware of this grace that's been extended to you, it may not change what you say but it will change *how* you say it.

You can be confident of this. We don't serve for grace. We serve from grace. We don't worship for grace. We worship from grace. We love people because God loves us not so that God will love us. It's from grace that we receive our calling, and it's from grace that we are able to serve the world around us.

I have banked my life on this. That Jesus plus nothing is better than everything minus Jesus. I believe every person on planet earth has the right to know Jesus and I want everyone to experience the same grace that's been extended to us.

It's true that we all go through valleys in life no matter if you love Jesus or not. You are either walking into a storm, you are in the middle of a storm, or you are coming out of a storm. Every one of us are going to experience challenges in life, but if you stay close to Jesus and run to Him, that valley you are walking through doesn't have to break you and it doesn't have to define you or make you its victim.

You have the right as a Christian to turn the page and start a new chapter in life and declare, "What I walked through made me more in love with Jesus and set me on a path for greater things to showcase Jesus to others."

Grace is so much better than what we deserve and greater than what we can possibly imagine. Jesus knew that it was okay to not be okay sometimes. He also knew that it wasn't okay to stay that way. So grace opened up room for truth.

The Bible says Jesus wasn't coming to bring a list of rules for change:

For the law was given through Moses; grace and truth came through Jesus Christ.

(John 1:17)

I am so thankful for God's grace every single day.

Are you willing to stay in the fight and keep showing up and serving people, even when they are at their worst? Are you willing to not throw in the towel on someone but keep believing the best in them?

I have found that people are more likely to change because another person believes in them and doesn't give up on them than when people don't believe in them and throw in the towel.

I want to remind you that Jesus believes in you and He's not giving up on you. No matter what you have done, you can never make Jesus love you any more or any less than He does at this very moment. He is not throwing in the towel on you. And we're not throwing in the towel on this generation.

Despite all the pain, heartache, and devastation we are seeing in our modern world, I love this generation and see great potential in it. I consider it an honor that God has planted us in this generation so others can be drawn into a relationship with Him.

> I remain confident of this: I will see the goodness of the Lord in the land of the living.

> (Psalm 27:13)

There hasn't been a better time to show grace to others and see people come to know Jesus than right now. Anytime Jesus shows up, grace and truth come with Him and that's how we should live and operate every day of our lives. We are called to be salt and light, extending grace everywhere we go, drawing the best out in people.

Because . . . if not us, then who?

4

for the culture

This was the most difficult chapter for me to write—not because it was hard, but because there is so much that needs to be talked about regarding what manhood really looks like through the eyes of a servant. This chapter could be an entire book!

It's so easy for women to share their feelings and deal with their emotions, but for men, we've trained ourselves to suppress feelings, rub some dirt on them, and move on. There's never been a time in history where manhood has been more misunderstood than right now. There is so much that we can speak into single men, and I hope if you are single reading this book, you learn some important lessons early on in life from this chapter. However, I'm going to be focusing on married men who are called to serve their homes God's way.

Before we dive into it, I want to take a moment and honor every husband and father reading this book who is doing everything he can to lead his family well.

I want to celebrate every man who is striving to live a life of purity in a world that is so perverse you can't even turn on your laptop without sexual ads popping up on every web browser you turn to.

I have the honor of being a husband and father of six kids. I want you to know that being a man in this day and age isn't for wimps. So I just want to applaud you men who have chosen to stay in the fight and continue to find ways to improve so you can lead from the front.

You are doing better than you think just by showing up every day choosing to become better today than you were yesterday. What I am going to share in this chapter are things I've experienced in my own life and things I've walked thousands of couples through over the years in ministry and things I'm still learning at my age.

Manhood seems to always be changing depending on what generation you are born into. It's changed so much even since I was a kid. I remember as a kid I would sit down with my grandpa and he would tell me stories of what manhood looked like from his set of lenses. It was the best. Both of my grandparents were 100% Italian who migrated to Chicago, Illinois on a boat when they were children. Their parents spoke Italian, they went to an all-Italian church, made 100% authentic Italian food, and only married Italians.

It wasn't the most inclusive generation we've ever known to say the least.

Still, my grandparents were my heroes. They passed away several years ago and there's not a day that goes by that I don't think about them and wish I could hear their voices again. But when I was a kid, I wanted to be around my grandpa all the time because he told the best stories of how tough he was as a young man.

My grandpa was always bragging about how tough he used to be in his glory days. He was this 5' 3" ball of energy and to him, being a real man meant your chest and back was full of hair, you worked hard for your family, and could melt your wife's heart singing in Italian. My grandpa told us at least a thousand times how, when he was a teenager, he laid on train tracks and wouldn't get up until my grandma agreed to go out with him on a date.

Any man who is willing to lie on train tracks for a woman deserves at least one date. If you fast forward, the next generation would give you a completely different answer as to what manhood really looks like.

I think the question needs to be asked: "What does real manhood look like in the eyes of God, and how does that picture compel us as men to lead with a servant's heart?"

I don't think there's one answer that fits all because all of us are shaped by different experiences—and by our own fathers who have impacted the lenses in which we view manhood.

However, there are glimpses in the Bible that allow us to see how God is calling us to be as men, glimpses that reflect His character and calling on our lives.

FATHERHOOD THROUGH THE EYES OF 2PAC

2Pac was not only a talented artist, but God also blessed him with an incredible mind to be able to put into words what many people were experiencing. He was part of a revolution movement in his time because millions of young men could relate to what he experienced. He told their story from the mind of one of the greatest rappers of all time.

He wasn't a pastor, but he was a preacher. And I assure you he was passionate about the message he was communicating.

I loved listening to his music because of the passion, authenticity, pain, and vulnerability he made you feel. He wasn't trying to write a polished song that someone else wrote that he was forced to perform. He rapped from a deep place of pain. He performed from a place that conveyed to the world what He believed to be true.

When he performed, he made you believe in every word he was saying.

He could write a hit that made you dance and on the next track he could make you feel hurt for what he's endured in life. I understand a lot of his songs are inappropriate, but his albums were snap shots as to why he was the way he was.

One of 2Pacs songs that moved me and gave me a different perspective about him was a song called Papa'z Song. You can Google the lyrics for yourself—but be cautioned, there are some pretty graphic words. However, when you realize what this man walked through, can you blame him? There is one line in that song that grabbed me.

With pain in his soul and passion in his voice 2Pac would deliver the line: "How can I be a man if there's no role model?"

That's a great question. 2Pac was begging for a man to be around that he could follow.

[Ladies, let me give you some quick insight about men before I speak to the men. God wired men to be driven, to be passionate, and to crave encouragement.

When a man feels like he is failing, it comes out in a number of different ways. I'm sure as a woman this sounds weird, but men thrive in an environment of encouragement. If you would speak life over your husband, he might want to come home a little more often. If you tell your man how strong he is at moving the boxes in the garage, he'll try to pick up three at a time just to impress you and pretend like it's nothing (even if he does pull a muscle in his back trying to impress you.) If you tell him how much you appreciate all that he does for the family, he may just plant that organic garden in the backyard for you.

My wife goes above and beyond to encourage me. Words of affirmation isn't my love language, but every man wants to know they are valued and respected. Every day my wife tells me how much she appreciates me and how proud she is of me. I don't really know what she sees in me.

Alicia is way out of my league and I'm really not as cool as she says I am. Love is blind, but you know what? I really do appreciate it.

Men thrive in an environment where they feel respected. Men aren't drawn to criticism. I know I'm going to be walking a very thin line in this chapter because there is a feminist movement in our culture that has been trying to demonize men and send a message to women that they don't need men. Every sitcom on TV is about exploiting how pathetic and incompetent men are, and that women are the ones that lead the homes.

But it was God's design to have men lead their home by calling them to a life of servanthood.]

And that's no easy calling. Especially when we are full of testosterone.

Men are aggressive, competitive beings. You can't take that out of us. Yes, we can control it and we learn to channel that energy, but it's wired into the fiber of our being. We want to win at everything we do. We want to win in our careers, in our marriages, even at video games.

I know some men are more competitive than others at certain things. I will admit, I'm highly competitive. I'm not competitive where I'm a jerk and try to show people up. I'm internally competitive. If I ran a professional sports team, I could never be the owner that tanks on purpose. It's not in me.

My kids love to play Mario Brothers on their gaming system. They love it. And I love it because I can channel my inner youth and go back to the old school Nintendo days and actually beat them.

My girls want to just have fun. My son and I want to win. I don't know where I get this aggravation and competitiveness to want to win something as ridiculous as Mario Brothers. It's not even about the game. It's about accomplishing what I set out to do.

When we have game nights, most of my kids are just as competitive as me. We play to win. I don't care who it is or what we are doing, if I have a chance to win, I'm going for it.

My wife and I were best friends before we started dating. One gorgeous day in San Diego, she felt brave to challenge me to play tennis. Apparently she thought because she played four years on the tennis team in high school that it gave her an advantage.

It makes sense. I've never played tennis besides a few times for fun. But I had a blast being with her, so I accepted the challenge.

She had this sexy-sporty look going on, but I knew in my head that as soon as she served the ball I couldn't let her win. If she did, I would never hear the end of it. It doesn't bring me great joy to say this but I won every set. Okay, maybe it brings me a little bit of happiness. I remember she was so mad.

We fell in love, got married, and before we knew it, she was nine months pregnant with our first child. Apparently the hormones were all over the place because she once again challenged me for a rematch.

Honestly, I tried to talk her out of it but she wasn't hearing any of it.

I know what you are probably thinking.

"Of course you let her win. She's nine months pregnant and is carrying your firstborn child."

I'm once again embarrassed to say that something inside of me just couldn't let her win. I told you, I'm not the tanking type. It's a blessing and a curse. I even started to have some fun with it by hitting the ball on the opposite side of the court just to see her waddle as fast as she could to get it. Don't feel too bad for her.

She's as competitive as I am. It was all in fun.

If you know Alicia, she will try to find whatever competitive edge she can to win. She held her belly, pretended like she was going into labor, and asked me to let her win one set before the baby came out. But I wasn't falling for that.

I just couldn't do it.

Men want to win. That is why my wife and I have a passion to build families. We want to see you win in the things that God values most. We want you and your family to get to the end of your life and say you built a home that will last for generations. How heartbreaking to work all your life for something only to find out it didn't really mean anything in the end.

LEARNING TO LEAD THROUGH STRUGGLE

Men, one of the greatest callings we have in this world is the privilege of serving our families. There are so many people who take shots at being a family man, but I want to tell you that being a husband and a father is a gift! I wouldn't trade my life with anyone.

That doesn't mean we don't have our struggles and we don't have bad days . . . sometimes we have bad weeks. Still, I tell people I'm living the dream and it has nothing to do with what I drive, what neighborhood I live in, or how much money is in the bank.

My wife and six kids are my best friends in the world. If I had a choice to be with anyone, I choose to be with them. In saying that, being a husband and a father is a real struggle at times. Men, we are in a fight for our lives and our homes every single day. This chapter wasn't written to try and paint a utopia version of life that isn't real. It was written to show you that it doesn't matter who you are or how much you love God, there are battles inside a man's heart that never seem to go away.

Issues of anger, lust, greed, selfishness, depression, and pride are waiting for us when we wake up every day. It's easy to fool ourselves into believing that if we really love God we won't have any more struggles.

The truth is, you can love God with everything inside of you and for the rest of your life still have struggles that always seem to knock at your door.

In our generation, when things get hard, we too often hear of men checking out and running away. Or they stay but are either emotionally checked out or start taking out their aggression on those they love most. I think one of the best ways we show what real manhood looks like is how we lead and keep serving our families when times are tough.

When I think of man serving his home in the Bible, one story that comes to mind is a man named Jacob. The name Jacob means "one who grabs." He was named this because he grabbed his brother Esau's heel when we was being born. Esau was born first. The firstborn in those days had the birthright, but Jacob grabbed onto his brother's heel when we was being born and thus stole the birthright.

Sounds like a typical baby brother.

Esau was Isaac's firstborn, but he lost his birthright to Jacob in one moment.

From that moment on, these two men's struggle never stopped.

Jacob grew up and the time had come for him to find a wife. So his father Isaac sent him away to find one. That means men need to get out of their mom's basements and learn how to become providers.

It was time for Jacob to leave and become man. So he left for his journey.

While he was still talking with them, Rachel came with her father's sheep, for she was a shepherd. When Jacob saw Rachel, daughter of his uncle Laban, and Laban's sheep, he went over and rolled the stone away from the mouth of the well and watered his uncle's sheep. Then Jacob kissed Rachel and began to weep aloud.

(Genesis 29:9–11)

Jacob was just like any man. He was trying to impress Rachel. He locked eyes on this beautiful woman and what did he do first? He moved rocks to show how strong he is. Remember, a man thrives in an atmo-sphere of encouragement. I can imagine Jacob probably took off his cloak, rolled up his sleeves and rolled that stone away by flexing a little more than he needed to. Then Jacob does something that showed how strategic he was on trying to win Rachel's heart.

Jacob started to serve. Jacob didn't roll the stone away and put up his feet and watch her do all the work. He didn't say, "I did my part now it's time for the ladies to do their part." No! Jacob started serving. Well played, Jacob. Well played. He took the role as the man and started to serve by watering Laban's sheep. Serving paved the way for intimacy.

Men, if you want to have a better sex life, it starts in the kitchen, not in the bedroom. It's time you stop complaining about not getting enough sex and start serving her by doing the laundry and picking up your dirty clothes. It's time you stop worrying about the needs you have and start serving her needs.

You want to have a great sex life?

Start helping out with the kids. Start coming home earlier to help out with dinner. Instead of heading straight to the couch after dinner, do the dishes and let her sit down. There is nothing sexier to a woman than a man vacuuming the living room. Can I get an "amen" from the ladies! If the kids are asleep, who knows! You might even get lucky with spontaneous sex. She might just tackle you in the middle of you vacuuming just because you are serving her.

It's great that you provide a paycheck, but that's the job God gave us since the fall of man. But if you want your marriage to go to another level, not just with your sex life, start serving.

Jacob started to serve Rachel and at some point, when he was watering the sheep he must have started to hear Luther Vandross singing "Wait for Love" from the hilltops because this dude got the urge to go in for a kiss.

Luther was one of the greatest singers of all time. He still moves my soul.

This part of the story reminds me of the pool scene on Sandlot when Squints pretends to drown just to kiss Wendy Peffercorn. Squints was my hero growing up. Every kid wanted to be him. That's the courage that is inside of a man.

Jacob's spontaneous kiss would have been the perfect moment that every man would have celebrated for a lifetime . . . if he didn't start weeping afterward.

I know there are many different interpretations on what manhood looks like from generation to generation. But I'm pretty sure every man can agree that weeping out loud after your first kiss is never okay. Ever!

After I kissed my wife for the first time, I looked at her like, "I know, right. Wasn't it awesome!"

Why?

That's what men do. We have confidence. Apparently this kiss that Jacob laid on Rachel must have been a pretty good one because it worked out. Rachel went home to tell her father, Laban, and instead of coming back to the well to beat him with a club, Laban invited him to stay with them.

In no time at all they fell in love.

Laban was an old-school dad. The terms to marry Rachel were steep. Jacob had to work for her father for seven years. My wife and I were best friends three years before we started dating. But when we started dating it took us three months to get engaged. When you know you just know. I can't imagine having to wait seven years.

Apparently Rachel was worth it to Jacob because he agreed to the terms. If you read the story, Jacob loved Rachel so much the time flew by. When the seven years were finally up, Jacob was ready to marry Rachel. However, Laban tricked Jacob. Because women had to cover their entire face, Jacob ended up marrying Leah his oldest daughter instead. Jacob was outraged. You can't blame him. He worked seven years not just for love . . . for sex, too.

Let's be real.

Jacob was ready to pop in the mixed tape and have Luther sing for their entire honeymoon. Can you imagine how outraged you would be if you were deceived like that? Next, Laban told Jacob if he wanted to marry Rachel, he had to work for him another seven years. I don't know many men who would have hung around and agreed to serve another seven years after being deceived like that.

Jacob was a real man. His love for Rachel burned so deep that he agreed to work another seven years just to be with her.

That's true commitment.

As men, when our hearts are engaged with something, we pursue it. Men are wired to be the pursuers. And once we reached that goal, it's so easy to lose our awe and wonder of what makes our wives so special like when we first met them. So many men stop pursuing their wives after they say "I do" and end up one day shocked that their spouses have emotionally detached from them or found acceptance in the arms of another man.

Our wedding day shouldn't be the end of pursuing our wives; it should be the starting point. It's so easy to let life, work, kids, and schedules rob us of our intimacy with our spouses, but as men, we should defend it with everything we have. There's not a day in our lives that we won't have something else to pursue instead of our families. There will always be something there to try and replace being present and involved with your family. We will never get enough sleep. We will never make enough money. We will never have enough time.

My wife and I want to keep dating one another. And to be honest, we haven't figured out yet how to make that more of a routine for us. It's something we are still working through together.

Let me encourage you to never stop pursuing your spouse. Never stop pursuing your daughters. Never stop pursuing your sons. Take your wife out on a date. If you have a daughter, set up daddy-daughter dates with her every month. If you have a son, set aside dude time every month to build into them the characteristics of what a man really is.

Choose your priorities wisely because they will define the health and spiritual destiny of your home. As the man of your house, you have to be attentive to what the spiritual atmosphere is. You have to sense when things are getting off track, when it's time to regroup, when it's time to pull things in and simplify life, and when it's time to move forward. It's your job as the husband to carry that responsibility. You have to be fully present.

And when I say present, I don't just mean you are in the room. Every man knows you can be there in body but absent in mind. I can't tell you how many times I have been in the family room with my kids while they are telling me about their day and at the end I had no idea what they were saying because I was thinking about something else.

Jacob was all in. We know from studying Jacob's life that he had some major issues he dealt with throughout his lifetime. He wasn't perfect by any stretch of the imagination. But when you read the story further, you begin to see cracks in Rachel as well.

It's funny how life works. When you are dating everything can seem perfect. You think everything she does is adorable—until one day you realize the things you use to think were adorable are the things you start to despise about her. I don't care how beautiful a woman is, they all have pain or insecurity in some way that they are carrying. And it's up to us as men to love our wives and daughters through that. You can't expect a woman to respond and carry pain like a man does. That isn't fair to her. Women aren't built like men. Thank God for that. God wired them completely different.

I see so many men trying to shut down their wives' emotions and belittle them when they start to express themselves and it builds walls, produces mind games inside of their heads that never used to be there, and creates more pain inside of their hearts.

As men we have a responsibility to nurture our wives and help them process what they are feeling. That's being a real man. That's called servanthood. It's not about trying to get them to be quiet so you aren't annoyed any longer. That's pride and selfishness. We serve our wives when we allow them to express what they are feeling and give them a voice in every matters of what happens inside of the home. We serve our wives when we create space for them to feel safe to not be ok sometimes. As men we love to fix things. Women don't need to be fixed. They need to be loved. They need to be heard. They need to know that they have a safe place to lean on when life hurts most.

Women are so much stronger than past generations gave them credit for. Women are strong, intelligent, driven, courageous, talented, and capable of birthing a human being from their bodies. I don't care how strong you think you are as a man. I'm telling you right now . . . they win!

Marriage is such a beautiful gift and should be a safe zone for our wives to express their deepest emotions without fear of being rejected.

Rachel had a secret pain that was very embarrassing in her day. She was barren. If you were barren in that time in history, it brought shame on you. If a woman was barren according to the ancient laws they were allowed to give their husband to their maidservant to provide a baby for them. Talk about adding to the pain and sense of rejection. Not only did they carry the pain of not being able to conceive, but now they have the pain of their husband being with another woman as well.

By this time, Jacob had kids with Leah, Rachel's sister, but he was in love with Rachel. I can only imagine the drama from being married to two sisters. I'll just leave it at that. But Jacob stood by Rachel through her pain. One day, God answered Rachel's prayer and she gave birth to a son. She named him Joseph. We'll talk about Joseph later in the book. Knowing what we know now, it's no surprise that Jacob loved Joseph with every fiber in his being.

Rachel would conceive again, but this time the pregnancy didn't go as well as the first one. This pregnancy threatened her life:

Then they moved on from Bethel. While they were still some distance from Ephrath, Rachel began to give birth and had great difficulty. And as she was having great difficulty in childbirth.

(Genesis 35:16–17a)

Ephrath is Bethlehem. Jacob was doing everything he could to get Rachel to Bethlehem. He loaded her up in that wagon and was going through the bumpy roads, muddy fields and doing everything he could to get her to Bethlehem. While Jacob was up front with the horses trying to get the horses to go as fast as they could, I imagine he heard Rachel's pain from the back of the carriage. As a man, you feel helpless in those moments.

Jacob—who at one time flexed his muscles by moving that big stone at the well to serve Rachel—found himself without enough money or muscle power to help her. That's a hard place to be for a man.

There was not a person in the world that Jacob loved more than Rachel. I can't imagine how loud he must have been praying for God to heal Rachel.

"Be strong, Rachel. We are almost there," Jacob must have said.

As a husband, I feel for Jacob. There is not a person in this world I love more than Alicia. Jacob doesn't have Uber to rush him to the nearest hospital. He doesn't have the luxury of having his wife airlifted to an Emergency Room. Jacob is in a wagon on bumpy roads serving his wife the best way he knows how in one of life's hardest moments, and it didn't have a happy ending.

As she breathed her last—for she was dying—she named her son Ben-Oni. But his father named him Benjamin. So Rachel died and was buried on the way to Ephrath (that is, Bethlehem).

(Genesis 35:18–19)

Rachel didn't make it.

She held on just long enough to hold her son for a moment and then passed away.

Jacob came up a little short.

Rachel was buried on the way to Bethlehem.

Men, there are times where we are going to come up a little short serving our families. I wish I could paint this perfect picture for you that if you love Jesus and do everything you are supposed to do as a man then everything will work out perfectly for you.

The truth is you can love God with all of you heart and do everything you are supposed to do and still come up a little bit short.

There is a righteous anger that rises inside of my soul when I hear people belittle fathers these days. I know the struggle and the burden of what fatherhood feels like. So many fathers are doing their best to lead with pressures on their shoulders that past generations didn't have to carry. So many fathers are trying to learn what it means to be the role model for their kids that they never had growing up. So many men are trying to relearn what it means to be engaged with their family because all they saw growing up was their dad working for their pension.

I have a passion to speak life into men because most of the men I run into are doing their best to be the best man they can be for their family. Even if you come up a little short, I want you to know that it's not the end. Keep moving forward. Your family is counting on you.

There's purpose in the pain.

SERVING WHEN YOU HAVE NOTHING LEFT

I wish I didn't have to say this statement, but there will come a time in your life where you have to keep serving your family even when you feel like you have nothing left to give.

I told you my fifth born, London, was born with some complications. Our other four babies had smooth deliveries. There were no signs of concern heading into the delivery room with London. I remember like it was yesterday. Everything went according to plan, and London was born full term. I felt like she was my firstborn all over again. The feeling never got old. I was just as in love with her as my other four the moment I laid eyes on her.

The doctor and nurses did their usual routines after a baby is born and everything appeared to be normal. When the nurses were taking London's measurements, they told us they had to take London to the NICU to get checked really quick, that there was nothing to worry about, and they would be back with her shortly.

Alicia and I didn't think anything of it. Alicia got some rest and I headed to a nearby pizza place to get some food. About thirty minutes later my wife called and said she was getting worried because they hadn't brought London back yet. With our other four, our babies never left the room. I could hear the nervousness in her voice so I headed back to the hospital right away.

We waited for a few hours to get some updates. We had that feeling you get as parents that something wasn't right. The nurses kept telling us that London was just getting used to breathing normal. So as soon as they allowed us to see London, we went back to the NICU and saw her getting oxygen.

It was a lot to process as we tried to figure out what was happening with her. She was making wheezing noises and you could tell that every breath was a struggle.

For the next thirty-six hours we were in the dark as to why she was in the NICU; we weren't told why she wasn't improving.

I'll never forget the feeling I felt when those doors opened in our hospital room.

The head neonatologist over all the NICU's over the entire Kansas City Metro area came in with her team behind her. That couldn't be good news. She sat down and I felt like all the air was sucked out of the room. I don't think we were ready for all that they were about to unload on us.

When she finished telling us the full scope of what London was up against, I'll never forget the sound of my wife's cry. I don't think I've ever heard so much pain in her voice in that moment. It was something I couldn't fix. I couldn't make it better for her. As a man, I was trying to hold it together for my wife but inside, I was hurting. I felt helpless.

All we wanted to do was go hold our baby girl. London must have felt so scared and alone in that NICU all by herself with strangers poking her with needles. That was our baby they were poking. It was my job as the man to protect her.

If you are a father, you understand what I'm talking about.

After Alicia and I took a moment to pray together, they informed us that needed to do a procedure where they would go through London's umbilical cord to run some tests. The nurses were running out of places to poke her because in one hand she had an IV and the other one was so black and blue from being poked so many times to get her levels.

It turned out that London had a surfactant deficiency, which means premature lungs. This surprised our doctor because her sonogram looked perfect and she had been developing right on track the entire pregnancy. London was a full-term baby and her lungs should have been developed by then. Surfactant is critical because it reduces the surface tension of fluid in the lungs and helps make the small air sacs in the lungs more stable. This keeps them from collapsing when an individual exhales. She also had pneumothorax, which occurs when some of the tiny air sacs in a baby's lung become overinflated and burst. It's very painful every time you take a single breath.

We would sit and watch our baby girl make this heartbreaking squealing sound every time she took a breath. The nurses couldn't even touch her she was in so much pain. If that wasn't enough she had respiratory distress syndrome because her lungs were caved in; she had to breathe so fast just to get oxygen. So she was on full oxygen with needles in her hands, inside her umbilical cord, both of her feet, and in her scalp.

And if that wasn't enough she got pneumonia, too, because she came out so fast that she swallowed fluid.

It felt like time stood still in that hospital room. We couldn't even touch or hold our baby girl. Alicia's parents would bring up our other four kids to see London and they had to look at her through a glass window. It just became a waiting game. If London's body didn't produce the surfactant there was nothing they could do.

Thankfully, my Blackhawks were in Game 7 of the Stanley Cup Finals, which helped to pass some time. London was my good luck charm because we won. I got to put the phone by her little ear in the NICU and she got to hear the celebrations.

They decided to take x-rays of London and all we could do was wait to see what to do next.

The head neonatologist over all the NICU's in the KC Metro area typically isn't even at our hospital. She just happened to be at the hospital we were at that day. Normally she is at the main hospital with the bigger NICU and she sees the reports from other hospitals through her computer screen.

It was such a God thing that she stayed with us because for two days she worked out of the hospital we were at and kept track of London.

I remember one time Alicia walked in to check on London and our neonatologist was standing over London starring at her, wondering what she could do next to help her. She had them roll in a ventilator because London wasn't getting better, but she didn't want to move forward with that quite yet.

Alicia asked why she was waiting to put London on a ventilator.

Our neonatologist said, "London's x-rays came back and if any doctor would have seen those x-rays they would immediately put this baby on a ventilator. Her lungs on her x-rays look awful. She is very sick. But when I look at her in person, she looks like she's holding on. Look at her. She fighting her way back."

When Alicia told me that, I knew London was a fighter.

I remember sitting alone in that hospital room and telling God that London was never ours to begin with. She belonged to Him and He entrusted her life to our care. So whether we were able to parent her for a lifetime or for a few days, we wanted to be faithful to fight for her. I wasn't really telling God anything He didn't already know; I was reminding myself of who was in control. I couldn't ever remember life without London. I loved her that much—and she was just a few days old.

In fact, even as I'm writing this part of the chapter, London is in my room by herself, playing cards, just hanging out with me. She's a feisty little thing. She's the only girl I know that bosses around her shadow.

But I remember I told God that day that whether He chose to heal London or not, I completely trusted His plan for her life. She was a gift given to us. So no matter what the outcome in this story would be, there was no way we would ever turn our backs on who He is. God could heal her with one spoken word. So whatever He was doing as we waited, we would choose to worship.

So we did. In that dark and cold NICU room we just prayed over her, played worship music in her crib, and read the Bible to her. We spoke the Word of God over her little life and began to speak out what we saw her becoming in this lifetime.

The hours seemed like weeks in that hospital room.

We would see little improvements that we would rejoice in and then there would be a complication and we would start praying. It was an emotional rollercoaster. And in the back of my mind, our four other kids were constantly in my thoughts. We were so blessed with so many people texting us Bible verses and friends who would message us saying they were worshiping and praying for our sweet baby.

I'll never forget the moment they allowed Alicia to hold London for the first time. London was connected to all her oxygen and was placed in momma's arms. Even as I write this I have tears. My heart couldn't take it the moment Alicia held London for the first time. She just clung to London and started crying. We would play the song "Cornerstone" by Hillsong Worship for hours and hours at a time believing that London would be fully healed.

There were many ups and downs during that week in the NICU, but by God's grace London began to fight her way back to the point where they could start feeding her through a feeding tube. She began to finally produce her surfactant and her body started to respond to the medicine for the other things she was facing.

One of the best days of our lives was when we got to bring London Joy home with us from the hospital. To say we celebrated would be an understatement.

For some people, this is a softball compared to what they've walked through in life. I get it. We've known people to walk through much worse that have cost them much more. We have walked people through some of the most heart wrenching things imaginable.

We're not trying to compare our story and make it any less or greater than anyone else's experiences. What I am saying is there are moments in life that are out of our control.

In those moments, our anchor better be tied to Jesus because those in our homes are counting on us to lead them through it. I've never felt more pain in my life than watching my wife's heart ache while our baby girl struggled to breathe. Little did I know that years later we would have to once again completely trust God as we watched our oldest daughter go through unexpected brain surgery.

If it had been one day later, my oldest daughter would be with Jesus right now.

Men, there are times in life where we have nothing left to give and yet there's a call on our lives to keep showing up to serve the best way we know how.

PROGRESS NOT PERFECTION

I think every man can feel what Jacob was feeling in some way or another. We have all come up a little short of what we set out to do at different moments in our lives.

As men the pressures of life can seem overwhelming at times can't they? We try to be the best provider that we can be. Then we come home and have to rush off to coach our kid's teams. On top of that, we have daughters waiting for us to fulfill our promise for daddy-daughter dates and sons asking to shoot hoops. When the kids go to bed, you start to hear about what bills need to be paid and what issues need to be fixed around the house. Then there's "those talks" because of the look you made at the dinner table that offend your wife. It is so easy to want to disconnect and shut down.

I know every man reading this understands what I'm talking about.

I can only speak for myself. As much as I love my wife and kids, and as much as I love pastoring my favorite church in the world, at times I wrestle with feeling like I'm coming up short. It's a personal struggle inside of me that I've recognized over the years and God patiently walks me through.

It's one of those things I have to constantly keep in check.

This battle—that may be with me for the rest of my life—constantly competes for my worship. It's the struggle of wishing I could give my family the world but many times feeling like I don't have enough or I am not enough. And as hard as I try, there is a feeling from time-to-time that I'm coming up a little short.

Maybe this is the first book you've read where you've heard this type of vulnerability from a leader. But it's true.

I'm sure I'm not the only man who has ever felt that way.

I want to encourage you with this. Your wife doesn't need the world. She needs just needs to know that she's your world. She needs to know that you are going to lead your family spiritually. Your kids don't need the college fund. That's great if you have that. But what they really need is to know that their dad adores and loves them more than life itself.

Your kids need to see you loving your wife and speaking life over her.

The best thing I can do for my church is to make sure I have a healthy marriage.

My family is my greatest ministry platform, not VIVE Culture. And the same goes for you wherever you are employed.

But remember, it's about progress not perfection. I am making a bold assumption but I am willing to bet most women would rather be in an average house on a tight budget and have their man home more and leading spiritually than have you gone all the time and you live in luxury.

✦[At VIVE Culture we have a passion to reach the men of the home.

Why? Because we believe if we can reach the man we can win the home.

Statistics show that if a church reaches the woman of the home, 13% of kids will become followers of Jesus. If a church reaches the man of the home, 93% of the kids will become followers of Jesus. Why? Because there is something so powerful that God set in motion when men lead their homes God's way.]✶

Men, be very careful that you don't say you are a Christian-centered family but with your energy, passion, resources, and time teach your kids that something else is. You can't expect your kids to have a passion for God and His Church when you are sleeping in every Sunday, out of town all the time, or have them signed up for sports all year long on the weekends.

How are your kids supposed to be engaged worshipers if you're in church, disengaged, just starring at the stage drinking your coffee? A man's countenance speaks much louder than his words sometimes. I can tell my kids I'm ok, but they know by my face if I'm really ok or not.

This one day I had a lot on my mind and my oldest daughter Kaitlyn asked, "Dad are you doing ok? Is something wrong?"

I responded like every guy and said, "Of course I'm fine."

She asked me again, "Are you sure dad?"

"Why are you asking me if I'm ok or not?" I snipped back.

"Because you are saying you are fine but your face is saying something entirely different," she replied.

How did my baby girl grow up so fast!

Kids can tell by our face what is really going on in our hearts.

How are our kids supposed to have a heart to serve if they don't see us making a habit of it?

Kids athletic programs, particularly in the Kansas City area, have become a god to thousands of people. And it's destroying homes. Competitive sports have overtaken thousands of homes and it's almost as if it's a badge of honor for parents to brag about how many games they have their kids in every weekend.

[When we fill our kid's calendars, we are promoting sports, or whatever else occupies peoples' Sundays, is central in the home. Then one day, parents are shocked when they wake and their teen is hanging with the wrong friends, making horrible life decisions, and wants nothing to do with God]

Your primary job as the head of the home is not to be your kids' best friend. My kids are my best friends and I tell them that all the time. [However, my primary role as the man of the home, before God, is not to bend to their desires but to do what's best for them.]

* We dictate what drives their lives, not them. My daughter asks me almost every night if she can have ice cream before bed. Almost every night without fail. As much as I love her, you would think I was an irresponsible parent if I let her. Why? Because that's unhealthy for her. Yet, we hear things like, "My kids are amazing at soccer and loves to travel on his competitive sports team. So we just don't have time for church," and somehow we think that's great parenting?*

[Something has become so twisted in our society. The enemy of our souls is out to destroy families and one of the ways he is doing that is through the businesses of our lives so we no longer have time for the things of God.

As the man of your house, you will stand before God one day and give an account on how you led your home. He's not expecting perfection but it is our responsibility to make progress.]

All have sinned and fall short of the glory of God.

(Romans 3:23)

We all have fallen short. Take the pressure off. There is no perfect man. God isn't looking for you to be perfect. When I start to take on too much pressure and feel like I'm coming up short, I remember that I don't have to carry the pressures alone. God is looking for us to take responsibility, to own our moment as the husbands and the fathers of our home, and lead in a godly way. There's a special grace for your life as the head of your home that God gives you to serve faithfully.

Men are goal oriented. We love to set a goal in front of us and meet that goal. You better have a clear understanding of what the win really is as the head of your home.

The most important goal for us as fathers isn't to raise well-behaved kids. The win at the end of the day isn't to get them into a great college or make sure they are in every sport on the weekends so they have a chance at a sporting scholarship.

If your kids grow up to be smart, well-mannered, successful adults but don't have a heart for things of God . . . you lose, and so do they. You are setting the pattern and priorities in their lives that will effect generations after you.

Every father's goal should be to serve his family by leading them to love and know the things of God before anything else. Jesus said:

But seek first his kingdom and his righteousness, and all these things will be given to you as well.

(Matthew 6:33)

That starts with your example.

I believe we can see God's idea of manhood come alive in a greater way in our moment in history. I have seen with my own eyes a generation of men rising up that lead their homes with passion in their soul for the things of God. I see a church full of men with their hands raised toward heaven and tears falling down their faces because they are so in love with Jesus. I see a church full of men using their gift to make money to build the God's house, not just build up their 401K. I see a church full of men loving their wives and speaking life and grace over them. I see a church full of men that isn't intimidated by a strong woman but makes room for her to shine.

I see a generation of men that don't have to sacrifice their manhood for bad hygiene. It's possible to smell fresh every day and still feel like a man. We are redefining what manhood looks like our generation.

I absolutely loved what Matt Chandler, Pastor of The Village Church said to men about serving their homes. He said,

"Husbands and fathers, when they come home, need to realize the hard work and challenges of their wives, as the mother of their children, and suck it up and serve their children and wives. They don't need to waste the evening watching TV or playing video games or endlessly surfing the internet. God has entrusted our wives and children to our care—we are their resident spiritual shepherds. One of the great ironies of the feminist movement has been, in the name of empowerment, to pressure women to take on the role of both father, provider, mother, and caregiver. They end up doing nearly everything.

Brothers, let's not waste our lives and fail our wives and children. Let's rise to the occasion and man-up, to the glory of Jesus, in a culture that has emasculated men and convinced us that our wives and children will do fine without our leadership and hard work."

To that I shout from the top of my lungs, amen!

Here is a great gauge as to what type of man someone is. If you want to know what kind of a man someone really is don't look at what they drive, where they work, or how much money they have. Look at his wife. There should be a countenance glowing on your bride because of the love they feel next to us as men. We should be paving the way for our wives to flourish in their gifts. We should be on the floor playing with our kids. We should go to bed exhausted from all that we have done to serve our home. Our daughters should feel empowered to stand up for themselves and be able to lead with confidence. Our sons should feel a responsibility to lead their homes in a godly way.

Our sons should feel an ownership to love and care for their mother. We should be reminding them daily that they are the future heads of their home.

Get rid of the score cards. Score cards are childish. Lead with love with no strings attached.

My wife is strong and courageous in her own right. She doesn't need me and yet God chose me to help lift her up!

Alicia is not *just* the pastor's wife. It's true, that's one of her roles but she stands strong alone without me. You get her passions stirring for building up women, families, and impacting our city and there's no stopping her.

Women have such an important God-given role and assignment in the home. That is absolutely true. In saying that, as men, you can't punt our responsibility as the spiritual leader of our homes and put that on our wife. That is our responsibility given to us by God. We can't say, "that's her thing to lead devotions with the kids, pray with them, and take them to church and my thing is to pay the bills and make sure all the vacation plans are set every year."

Our primary role as the spiritual head of the homes is to serve our family by leading them spiritually. We will stand before God and give account to that.

Let me encourage you to lead from the front by getting involved. You be the one waking your kids up on Sunday's and being excited to be in church. You be the ones where they look over and your hands are in the air, singing your heart out to the One who saved your soul. You be the one to teach them about being a faithful tither. You be the one that signs your family up to serve.

Your kids are smart. They know when you love something and when you are just doing it for your wife. You can't be an insanely obnoxious fan at a sporting event and when you are at church you are dead as a door-knob. Men, we get excited about things that have captured our hearts. If you don't believe, just watch people at a concert or sporting event. Our engagement has nothing to do with a personality type. It has everything to do with what has our hearts affections.

There is an authority that God has placed on your life as the head of the home that can't be carried by anyone else.

Our families are not a distraction from more important work. Men, they are the most important work.

Our families are our biggest ministry platform.

You have it in you. I believe in you.

And one of the best ways we can lead our kids is by serving our wives.

If you want to have a healthy, spiritual home, you have to serve your wife joyfully. You are not at your best when you are leading a board meeting making millions of dollars for your company. As a man, you are at your best when you are on the couch folding laundry with your wife. You are at your best when you take time to read the Bible with your kids, or throw them up in the air in the pool.

[Your kids will always love their mother, but they will always follow your lead.] It's time we kill the peter pan syndrome that's plagued us for far too long. Don't be the man who refuses to grow up. Take your place. Embrace your calling. Don't do life alone.

[And let me just add this in...you will never get from your wife or kids what you can only get from Jesus. As much as I love my family, they will never be enough. Only Jesus can fill that role. I'm not looking for my wife or kids to fill a void in my heart that only Jesus can fill.]

Get around other men who have a passion for their families, who are generous with their resources, and have a vision for their lives. It will change how you serve when you start to surround yourself with other men who serve. When you surround yourself with spoiled boys, you start acting like that.

You are who you surround yourself with.

If all you hang around is boys who buy expensive things and live for themselves, those are the lenses you will see life through. If you hang around men who live to serve their family and others through what they have been given, that is how you will live as well.

Men who refuse to grow up is only funny when we are watching it through the eyes of Everybody Loves Raymond. It's funny when Raymond doesn't want to watch his kids or help out around the house. It's heartbreaking when real life husbands don't want to. Father's when your wife is out with her friends and you are home with the kids, you are never, ever babysitting. It's called parenting!

So you are telling me that when mothers are home with the kids it's called motherhood but when fathers are home with the kids it's babysitting? We can kill that nonsense right now.

You are not a man because you can shave. You are man when you own the call that has been placed on your life to serve your wife and kids with every fiber of your being.

You are more capable than you think you are. I'm convinced that if you really want to do something well, you will find a way to make it happen. If you don't, you will think of every excuse why you can't. It's all about priorities. You are not incompetent. You are gifted. You are strong and you are called.

Your number one priority is not to your organization, your mortgage or even your kids. Your number one priority after your relationship with Jesus is your wife. It should go your relationship with Jesus, your spouse, your kids, your vocation and then sports.

I'm sort of kidding about sports.

REDEFINING MANHOOD

Like I said earlier, the definition of manhood has been greatly distorted. For generations, men have bought into the idea that being a man is how many beers you can pound, how many girls you can sleep with, how much weight you can bench, or how much money you can earn.

I love this verse that gives us an inside look at God's definition of manhood.

After removing Saul, he made David their king. God testified concerning him: 'I have found David son of Jesse, a man after my own heart; he will do everything I want him to do.'

(Acts 13:22)

At the end of my life, I only care about one thing written on my tombstone: a man after God's own heart.

That's really the goal.

It's not to be a great husband . . . although it's important to be one.

It's not to be wealthy . . . although there's nothing wrong with achieving that.

It's not to be a great person . . . although that certainly is important.

The goal is to be a man after God's own heart.

David was a man's man.

He was a warrior.

He killed a bear and a lion.

He spoke well.

He was good looking.

He was creative.

He was a musician.

He was in love with the Lord.

He was passionate.

He danced unapologetically in front of everyone when God's glory was returned to His people.

And get this...David even lived in community with other men.

That's right! David had thirty men who he lived in community with. These men were called David's mighty warriors. That means they weren't complaining about hard work and they weren't living in isolation. His mighty men weren't boys who could shave. They were men. So many of the hurdles guys face is because of their own circle of friends. You are who you hang around.

David's men were loyal, responsible, skilled, and faithful. They were my type of guys.

David was a man after God's own heart.

What made David so special? Let's face it. David was far from perfect. He lied, committed adultery, and was a murder. How could this man be labeled a man after God's own heart?

It's found at the end of that verse that we just looked at:

He will do everything I want him to do.

(Acts 13:22b)

David wasn't perfect. Nobody is. I hope you feel a weight is lifted off of your shoulders. We're going to make mistakes. But David loved God and always found a way to come back and do everything God asked him to do.

Everything that God asked David to do, he did it.

David loved to be in the House of God. He made sure his family was planted in church and he raised his kids to love the ways of God above anything else. David understood the principal of generosity and declared that he wouldn't give God a sacrifice that cost him nothing. In other words, he didn't take God's money that was set apart for Him and spend it on other things. That's robbing God and His House. David led in generosity and went above what was required of him.

Men, it's time we lead the way in our finances and show our families what matters most to us.

David also was a man who understood how to honor his leaders even when the leaders over him didn't deserve it. He just continued to serve. What I also love about David is he understood what he was fighting for not simply what he was fighting against.

There is a big difference.

What am I trying to say?

God's idea of manhood is someone who lives, leads, and serves God's way. Let's break the mold on what manhood looks like in our generation.

But if serving the Lord seems undesirable to you, then choose for yourselves this day whom you will serve, whether the gods your ancestors served beyond the Euphrates, or the gods of the Amorites, in whose land you are living. But as for me and my household, we will serve the Lord.

(Joshua 24:15)

I pray that the ways of the world become less desirable and the ways of God become the most desirable thing that we treasure. I'd love for every single one of us to get to the end of our lives and people say, "He was a lot of things. But what can sum him up best was he was a man after God's own heart."

FOR THE CULTURE

We have a saying at VIVE that we use. The saying is: for the culture. Basically what it means is you are requesting that someone carry out a specific action for benefit of their shared culture.

As men, we want to break the mold and make this type of living our culture as men in our generation.

Let's make a commitment to one another not to be *that* guy that works all day and then comes home and insinuates that his job is done because he's been working all day.

As the man of your home, it's your duty to work all day for your home. Your privilege is to serve your home. To imply that your job is done because you walk in the door and your wife's is to just keep going through the rest of the day taking care of the kids, running them to all their practices, on top of cooking, giving the kids baths, cleaning the house and so on is a very childish, un-biblical perspective on what it means to be a man. Sometimes your wife needs a little bit of grace to be able not to have the house perfectly clean for you because she's been investing in the kids all day.

When you get home, be all there. You be the one to speak out spiritually in your home. You set up a routine of family devotions, pray with them and tuck them in bed. At the dinner table, don't sit there quietly. Turn off your phone, and ask them questions about their life. Find ways to bring God into the situation.

Love God, your God, with your whole heart: love him with all that's in you, love him with all you've got! Write these commandments that I've given you today on your hearts. Get them inside of you and then get them inside your children. Talk about them wherever you are, sitting at home or walking in the street; talk about them from the time you get up in the morning to when you fall into bed at night. Tie them on your hands and foreheads as a reminder; inscribe them on the doorposts of your homes and on your city gates.

(Deuteronomy 6:5-9 MSG)

When dinner is over, don't just run to your phone, turn on the TV and check out. Help with the dishes and ask your spouse how she is doing. Listen to her. Don't make sarcastic comments and talk down to her. Build her up. Brag about her often. Extend grace when she comes up short. Serve her.

The greatest gift we can give our kids is loving their mother.

Understand that it's some much more important what you leave in your kids than what you leave to your kids. Leave them a godly legacy to follow in.

Let's commit to one another to be *that* guy. There's not a woman in the world that enjoys lying about what a great dad and husband they are married to. I know the pressures of life are enormous and exhausting. Let that push you towards Jesus. You will feel burn out if your life isn't tied to His heart.

My wife has learned how I am wired. Every day I try to give it my all. On the way home, that's my refreshing time. I turn off the radio and it's just quiet. And as I pull in the driveway I know that my day has not ended but my real job has just begun. That doesn't mean I'm not tired or I don't have bad days because I do. Trust me! I go through funks where my wife tells me to go catch a movie alone and come back with an attitude adjustment.

But we have to constantly be keeping our spirits fresh and hearts right to come home and serve well.

True rest isn't going to be found on a vacation. I have six kids. We don't take vacations; we go on trips together. We love it, but we come back exhausted. True rest that refreshes the soul only comes when we spend time with Jesus every day.

My goal is to walk in the door and let me wife and kids know they are the best thing I've seen all day. I put my bag down and whatever the kids are doing or whatever my wife is needing my goal is be all there. If you see your wife has had one of "those" days, take the kids and tell her to go take a hot bath and relax. If you come home and the kids are outside playing hoops, ask if you can jump in the next game.

Every day I do my best to try and check on the hearts of my kids. I ask them questions about school, their friendships, and how they are feeling.

Don't assume that your kids are just going to pour out their hearts. It's up to us as the spiritual authority over them to draw it out in them and be that man they know they can go to when they feel alone, scared or insecure.

Don't assume that your wife and kids know how you feel. I don't care if words of affirmation aren't your "love language." I pray you hear my heart when I say with all the love in my heart...GET OVER IT! If it matters to you, you will figure it out. If it matters that much to you, you will make it work. Stop starving your wife emotionally and spiritually because it's not your "gift" to speak life over her but then suddenly you have more than enough energy at night wanting sex.

[There is not a person on the planet that should encourage and love your family more than you.]

Trust me, if you make the investment now when your kids are young they will want to be around you when they grow up. I'm around couples older than me that made the investment into their marriage and when their kids left the house, they still had a great life to look forward to with one another. Their kids were a big part of their life but they never were their life.

It's about right priorities.

I love my parents. But I want to have a very different relationship with my wife and kids than what I saw growing up. So my wife and I are doing everything we can to put in the time and investment to create the home we feel is best for us so we can reap the fruits of that labor later in life.

By now you already know what I think about my wife. She's a superhero. At times I don't think she's human. I never realized how much she did until she went on a trip with her sisters and left me home with our six kids. I had to take over the role of homeschooling our kids, cleaning the house, and taking care of our baby boy in the middle of the night.

I have never appreciated her more in my life. It's easy to get used to seeing our wives thrive in their calling that if we are not careful we can take it for granted. But it's not just celebrating their skill sets. Men, we serve our wives by including them in our decisions.

I've seen so many men praise their wives for being a good mom but demonize them when it comes to the finances of the home. You may make millions of dollars in your company, but it is an honor thing when you bring your spouse in on important decisions of the home and ask for her input. When you are making a big decision like buying a house, moving, career changes, and so on, it may be your expertise, but it's your job to bring her alongside of you in the decision making process.

Early on in our marriage, I was so used to doing things on my own that I didn't value Alicia's input at all. I'm embarrassed by it now but every time she tried to share her thoughts on money, ministry decisions, or things she was feeling, I disregarded it.

When others would say the same thing I would lean into it but when she would, it didn't carry the same weight. I never meant to do that. Her voice just became normal that I didn't take time to value her thoughts. I'm still not perfect at it. Thankfully I married a gracious and loving person. Once a month we try to sit down and reconnect and make sure that we are on the same page with all the different areas we are responsible for.

Over the years I've learned that my wife brings a lot more than just being a great mom or wife to the table. Alicia is fun, incredibly gracious, and loves to be around people. When she walks in a room, she has one of those personalities where she lights up a room with her spirit. She also is incredibly smart, is great with numbers, is a visionary, and has wisdom beyond her years. She co-pastors VIVE Culture with me and is incredibly gifted at it. I love to watch her thrive. She has such a deep sense of discernment and is one of the most gifted people I know when it comes to building relationships. She has such a passion to build up women and speak life into moms. And 98.9% of the time when my wife feels something, she is usually on to something.

My wife doesn't need another dad in her life. She needs a husband. She needs a partner in life. Men, commit right now to being the kind of man that can one day stand before God and hear Him say, "Well done."

And if you didn't learn anything at all in this chapter, never forget that if you want to have an amazing sex life, start doing a couple loads of laundry without her asking. But the key is to make sure you crank up Luther Vandross in the background and she sees you putting in a load. That's the trick.

You are welcome ahead of time.

5

staying faithful in the mundane by Alicia Rose

At times my life feels like the movie Groundhog Day. I wake up, feed the kids breakfast, homeschool my kids, clean up the house, make dinner for my family, and get the kids ready for bed—and at the end of most days, I am still wearing the sweats I slept in the night before. I am living my dream of being married to my dream man and being the mother of my favorite six kids in the world.

As a little girl I always dreamed of being a wife and mother. All I thought about was how many kids I was going to have, what their names would be, what my wedding would be like, and living in a house that cleaned itself—because really, what women wouldn't want a house to clean itself?

As I got older, God began to put more dreams in my heart that I wanted to accomplish, but nothing came close to wanting to be a wife and mom.

But let's be honest ladies, no matter how much we love our husbands and kids, there are days where I want to run for the hills. When you have a baby that won't sleep through the night and you are living on 45 minutes of sleep, you don't feel the joy of the Lord. By now you know that Brian and I are just going to keep it real. Not every day is sunshine and roses.

Girls, we can be emotional sometimes.

There are days where the house is a mess, the kids smell like dog breath mixed with sweat and dirt, I'm all tapped out of ideas of what to make for dinner, and I don't care. I want to honor all the wives and moms who are reading this who are doing everything you can to serve your families. It's not easy.

Being a wife and a mom is one of the greatest honors we could ever have.

And it's exhausting.

One of my greatest passions is to build up women and moms and I have realized that twenty-first century women are exhausted. And if that isn't enough, we have the pressures of comparing ourselves to every other wife and mother on this thing called social media.

It's the best and worst thing that has happened to us. Not only do we have all the emotional insecurities that we wrestle with naturally as women, but now we have a platform that confirms those insecurities by seeing every other person's perfect life. I believe the emotional health of any woman is so important to how we serve our homes and how we serve others.

If you aren't healthy, you will have nothing left to give.

So often we give our best to things that don't really matter and end up giving the leftovers to the things that matter most. It's so easy to do.

I keep busy in life.

I'm pastoring VIVE Culture with my husband, and I'm the mother of six kids and have the privilege of homeschooling them. I love it. I really do. Most days it's a blessing. But there was one particular season when I was trying to teach my second born, Makayla, how to read and some simple math addition. I thought that was going to be the death of me. Makayla is very smart and she is such a natural leader and caregiver. She just makes things happen. So I was confused why she was having such a hard time with school. We would go over the same thing, again and again, and nothing would stick. I assumed it was just because she was being lazy. It didn't help that my oldest daughter was not only a great reader, and caught on to new things quickly, but she's ultra-competitive—just like her dad.

I thought I was a patient person until I had to teach Makayla how to read. God bless our elementary teachers who do this for a living. I was going to lose my mind. I was trying everything I could with her and nothing was working. It would be hard enough if I just had to teach her, but on top of that I also had to teach my other kids their subjects, too. I could tell that Makayla started to realize how far behind she was in reading. We could see her level of confidence drop; she hated school, and she began to confess things over her life like, "I'm just not that smart."

Once she started to believe that, her behavior changed and she started to give up on her schoolwork altogether.

As her mother, that one statement tore my heart apart. Makayla was very smart, but her view of herself killed her spirit to want to take another step forward.

As women, if we feel insecure or feel like we are failing, it's easy to want to give up. My young daughter was feeling so defeated and I was struggling to find the answer to help her.

So I did what any good wife does when they are having a meltdown. I texted my husband a long dramatic text venting my frustration. I can only imagine his face as he sat in his meeting reading it. I had every type of emoji face you could put into that text message. As a man he was probably confused as to what kind of emotion I was experiencing:

Was I sad? Was I mad? Was I confused? Was I hysterical?

Yes! *All of the above.*

I am a woman—and sometimes women have every emotion at once.

I'm surprised Brian wanted to come home knowing what he was walking into.

When he did, like a good man, he tried to take the kids to give me a break.

But I'm a talker. I love to talk things out. So Brian listened.

However, Brian—God love him—does what men are wired to do: fix things. Brian is a problem solver. That's what he does. As I was telling him about my day all over again, because I need to talk things out, I could see the wheels turning in his head. I assumed he was judging me. I was already feeling like a failure and now I had to deal with his assumptions about what he thought about me, too?

So I made the mistake of asking, "What are you thinking?" Brian made the mistake of answering honestly.

Don't ask Brian anything if you don't want an honest answer.

It wasn't the time or the place for him to begin to tell me what I could do differently to help Makayla feel more comfortable so she could become a better reader.

That thoughtful suggestion didn't go over like Brian thought it would. God bless that man but the last thing in the world I wanted to hear was how I could improve as a teacher from someone who had never walked in my shoes before.

He is a fast learner. Since that time, when I've had those days, he just listens quietly. Bless his little heart. I have learned that for some things I just have to call one of my sisters and talk it through because they are in the same season of life as me and they get it.

I love my husband, but there are times that no matter what you say to your man, only a woman can really understand what you are going through.

There is a beautiful story in the Bible about a mother, Naomi, and her daughter-in-law, Ruth. Naomi was a woman who had lost everything. Her future seemed hopeless and in the moment, it looked like she had nothing left to live for. Naomi was in such a bad place in life that she actually changed her name to a Hebrew name that means "bitterness" because that's what she was feeling.

It may have been a different time in history, but we do the same thing today. I hear so many women attaching labels to themselves that were never intended for them. They attach their circumstances to their identity.

Naomi, in this dark season she was walking through, didn't need a man to come rescue her. What she needed was another godly woman who could understand her pain and emotions to help walk her through it. And that's just what happened. The woman who came into her life was a woman by the name of Ruth—who happened to be her deceased son's wife.

Ruth changed the course of Naomi's life just by her words. She realized that Naomi had taken on a name that wasn't meant for her. She saw that she wasn't living up to her fullest potential.

We all have that ability inside us to build one another up and champion each other. Ladies let's stop competing with one another but instead start speaking hope into those hopeless situations to set one another up to win.

We all need a friend like Ruth. Ruth was committed.

I'm sure there were times when Naomi was draining. In fact, Naomi didn't want to burden Ruth with her problems and tried to get Ruth to go away and get on with her life. Naomi thought she had nothing left to offer. She had no sons to marry, no finances, and nothing left to give.

Ruth could have taken that as a sign to get out of town. However, Ruth had a loyal spirit. Notice how she responded:

Don't urge me to leave you or to turn back from you. Where you go I will go, and where you stay I will stay. Your people will be my people and your God my God.

(Ruth 1:16)

Can you imagine how Naomi felt in that moment?

I can't imagine what that must have done for Naomi's confidence, knowing that she had a friend who wasn't in it for what she could get but for what she could give. That's a real friend. Ladies, be that for each other. Be the one that speaks truth and life into situations that society tries to portray as a burden or annoyance.

My daughter, Makayla, was starting to attach labels to herself based on her circumstances. And I was called to be a Ruth to her and show her that she is not what her circumstances define her. She is smart, capable, and has incredible potential inside of her. Every single one of us can be a Ruth to someone throughout the day.

I meet so many ladies who have a negative view of what it means to be a wife and mother. I truly believe it's not because they want to carry that spirit but because life is hard. Life isn't a fairy tale. There are seasons where we feel incapable, lonely, and afraid of the unknown. There's not a woman on this planet that at one point or another doesn't feel like they aren't enough for their husband or family.

Those labels that battle for our affections every day can—if we aren't careful—begin to seem like truth. That's why it's so important to stay planted in the local church and around a group of friends who are willing to stand by you on the bad days as much as they would on the good days. I want you to know that a rough day or even a rough season does not dictate and define your future.

God has a huge plan for your life. Not someday. I'm talking about right now.

It's okay not to be okay sometimes, but that's where the encouragement of other godly ladies is so important to have around you. Because when we are healthy and feel confident in what we are doing, it's reflected in how we serve others. When we aren't, we begin to close up and become self-consumed with nurturing all the negative thoughts we have about ourselves and we miss out on what God wants to do in and through our lives.

We all have different dreams. For some women, it is to own a business. For others, it is to be in the corporate world. Some women have always dreamed of being a teacher or speaking to thousands of people at conferences. Regardless of what we dreamed of as little girls, as we get older, we go through different seasons where time stands still and we wonder: *Is there more to life than what we are experiencing?*

NOT NOW DOESN'T MEAN NOT FOREVER

Years ago when Brian and I were first married I loved being a part of church ministry with him. I loved pouring into people and speaking life into them. However, when we started to have kids, there was a season I had to step back. We were growing our family fast and when they are little, kids need every ounce of you.

I wasn't able to keep up and do both well. If you have kids you know that when kids are little it's a twenty-four-hour calling. You are constantly feeding them, wiping their bottoms, and being touched all the time—you can't even go to the bathroom without being disturbed. Your space is completely invaded. And I wouldn't trade that for anything in the world.

I meet so many wives and mothers and my heart just breaks for them. There is so much untapped potential in this generation of women. Ladies, you are brave, strong, and intelligent.

The enemy is selling so many lies to the women of our generation. Some of those lies are that you have to have everything your parents have right now, or that one blogger on Instagram has the cutest style and you need to go buy that outfit tomorrow. So we exhaust ourselves and spend ourselves into debt trying to keep up with what everyone else is having. Our husbands end up trying to keep up with all the house remodel shows that are so popular and, as a result, it leaves us emotionally drained, discontent, and financially strapped.

Another lie I see so many buying into is the poor-me mentality. The enemy is creating such a martyr spirit within women to constantly complain about everything in life.

I know there are days—even seasons—that are hard. I get it. I have six kids but sometimes we just need to suck it up. Every woman needs to have that friend in their life they can vent to and pour their heart out to from time-to-time. But that can't be a way of life.

One of those people for me is my sister Katie. She's my best friend, loves Jesus, and we know we can be completely vulnerable with life, marriage, and parenting, and it's a safe zone. When we go to each other's house, she knows that my home is the place where all the guards can come down and we can just be us.

We push each other to keep being better and I'm so grateful for her.

And when I need a kick in the pants, or vice versa, she does that to me, too.

Another person I have in my life like that is my mom. My mom is one of my heroes. My mom and dad raised ten kids, on one income, and when my youngest brother went to kindergarten, she went back to school to become a hospice nurse. I never heard my mom ever complain about being tired, not having enough money, or how hard her life was.

We weren't rich by any means growing up. But we never knew it. I loved my life.

I never even knew we were on a tight income. My mom always made time for all of us. When she was in school she would study at night when everyone was asleep so it didn't take away from her family time. Those are the kind of women I try to surround myself with. You are who you hang around. If the only women you hang around are women who cut down their husbands, talk about how hard their life is as a mom, or complain about how broke they are all the time, then you will take on that spirit.

If you are around moms that constantly talk negatively about motherhood, it will impact how you view motherhood.

If you only hang around women who talk about vacations, how discontent they are, or how annoying their kids are, you will take on that spirit, too.

Similarly, who you are attracts others.

Do not be misled: "Bad company corrupts good character."

(1 Corinthians 15:33)

You have to plant in environments that will produce in you the fruit to serve others well. If you plant in environments that see being a wife and a mom as a privilege, you'll begin to see it as that, too.

That's why when we set out to plant VIVE Culture we were committed to pastoring a family church. We know that when families plant in the right soil, it not only changes their lives, but it changes their family dynasty as well.

My mom was a great example of serving her home with the kind of spirit that is now impacting my home today. What was the secret that allowed my mom to serve her family with such an amazing spirit?

It was anchored in her relationship with Jesus.

Every morning my mom took time to read her Bible and pray. It was as if that was her time to recharge. She prioritized her quite time. She pursued Jesus when no one was watching and she knew she couldn't get through the day without it. So many times I would walk in and see my mom worshiping or reading her Bible, and it spoke volumes to me. I will never forget those moments and the impact it had on my own life. My mom would tell you she made mistakes and wasn't perfect. No one is. But she remained teachable and always taught us that without Jesus, we have nothing.

There is something that the presence of God does inside a woman's heart that nothing else can do. When you spend time every day with Jesus, it begins to clarify what your purpose is as a woman. My mom knew that she had only one chance to raise us.

I remember years ago when we had three babies under the age of three and it was a busy season to say the least. Ecclesiastes 3 talks all about seasons:

There is a time for everything, and a season for every activity under the heavens.

(Ecclesiastes 3:1)

There is a season for everything and I chose to embrace the season I was in as a young mother and give it everything I could. Did I have other dreams? Of course. God wasn't telling me that I would never be able to do those other things. He was just saying, "Not right now." I was in a different season.

Even Jesus recognized there were different seasons to His ministry. He would say things like, "The hour has come," signifying that an old season had ended and a new one was beginning. When Jesus was twelve years old in the temple, He could have launched His ministry—but it wasn't the time.

However, when Jesus did launch His ministry, the world saw miracles it had never seen before. He could have used that as a reason to stay around a little longer. People were getting saved. Families were being healed. However, He recognized the hour at hand and knew that the cross was the only way for humanity to be reconnected to God's heart.

[It's so important to not resist seasons but understand them so you can flourish in them.]

My greatest calling wasn't to a church; it was to my home. My kids weren't a distraction from ministry. They were the ministry and the greatest ministry platform I will ever be entrusted with. <u>If I was successful in church ministry, but failed my home, I simply failed.</u>

I understood that the years of watching my kids grow up would go by too fast. And they have. Now my kids are serving in the church we planted and my oldest daughter interns for my husband from time-to-time because she feels a call to ministry.

When I finally embraced the season I was in as a young mother, I realized my life wasn't over. It was just the beginning. Just because I wasn't in the day-in-and-day-out of church ministry, the truth was, I was in ministry by learning how to serve my family.

That was the best thing that could have happened to me because I realized how much I could accomplish.

I see so many young mothers make the mistake of compartmentalizing everything in their lives. They box everything in. Trust me, if you do that, eventually those boxes will start competing against one another. I remember when Bobbie Houston, co-pastor of Hillsong Church, shared how she and her husband, Brian, were able to accomplish so much in life and ministry.

[She talked about how they did life together and allowed everything to flow together. Yes, there are busy seasons, but when you are in it together it becomes a joy, not a burden. Our home is an example that they are absolutely correct.]

Don't revolve your entire life around your child. You are only setting yourself up—and your child—for a hard life.

[Please hear my heart. I think that once young couples have kids they often forget that their kids are *part* of their life—but they are not their *entire* life. When you make your kids your entire life, your priorities are all out of place. You stop dating your spouse and you miss the joys of just being together. When your marriage is healthy, you are able to pour into your kids the way only a woman can.]

I love my kids, but we don't revolve everything around their comfort. It doesn't matter if you have one kid or a dozen, you can't revolve your life around their preferences. We have seen too many kids who aren't able to adapt in life because their parents were so locked into their children's routines that they can't function.

THAT'S KEY ↙ Sometimes Brian and I will mess up our kid's routines to force them to learn how to adjust. ✱

Not only does that teach them how to be flexible but it teaches them how to serve one another. Kids these days just don't know how to serve. That's not their fault. That's on us. We have to be brave enough to push them out of their comfort zone and teach them to think about others before themselves.

✱ If you've gotten anything at all out of following Christ, if his love has made any difference in your life, if being in a community of the Spirit means anything to you, if you have a heart, if you care—then do me a favor: Agree with each other, love each other, be deep-spirited friends. Don't push your way to the front; don't sweet-talk your way to the top. Put yourself aside, and help others get ahead. Don't be obsessed with getting your own advantage. Forget yourselves long enough to lend a helping hand. ✱

(Philippians 2:1–4 MSG)

That type of spirit is taught long before it is caught. I love serving and supporting my husband. Brian is incredibly talented at so many things. He is one of the most even-keeled leaders you will ever meet. He is an amazing communicator and a gifted musician.

Me . . . not so much.

I can do a great triangle, but even so, I think I may be a little offbeat.

For the last decade my husband has been a worship pastor and I was trying to see where I fit in to it all. I couldn't sing or play an instrument. I didn't feel like the greatest communicator. I felt out of place, like I didn't have anything to give. I felt like the ministry side of me was slowly dying. I had no one to look up to and no one pouring into me. I would try to get fed from other places just to keep from losing my vision for what I knew God had called me to do. I was looking for something big I could do. Something important. What I didn't realize was what I was doing was important. God was teaching me to be faithful with what I was given and the opportunities I was given, no matter how big or small.

In Matthew 25:14–30, Jesus told the parable of the talents. We learn that one man received one talent, the other two talents, and the other man five talents. The two individuals that were given two talents and five talents went out and doubled theirs. On paper it may not have looked like the five had accomplished more; however, they both brought back one hundred fold.

It's about faithfulness.

The one that was entrusted with one talent did nothing. He buried it.

I find that so many women come to a season in their life and bury what is inside of them.

God isn't expecting every lady to do the same thing. He's not expecting every mom to homeschool their kids or have a big family. He's not expecting every woman to be in the corporate world, and not every married couple is called to have kids. God gifted you with specific things I'll never be able to do. But we are all called to do something with that gift. You and I are called to be fruitful with whatever God has entrusted to us.

God always calls us to do something with what we've been given.

This goes back all the way to the garden of Eden in the book of Genesis.

As a parent, I can imagine the joy on God's face the first time He laid eyes on Adam in the garden of Eden. Most people think the first command God gave Adam was to not eat the fruit from the tree of the knowledge of good and evil. But this wasn't the first command. Oftentimes the world paints this negative picture of God up in heaven trying to take away all of our fun. God is a loving Father. If we as parents want good things for our kids, and we are broken and flawed, how much more does God want good things for us as a perfect Father?

The first command God actually gave Adam was to be fruitful and multiply:

[God blessed them and said to them, "Be fruitful and increase in number; fill the earth and subdue it."]

(Genesis 1:28a)

The first command God gives humanity is to have sex.

That's right. How many times at the end of the day are we worn out with food or spit up on our clothes, and the last thing we want to do is have our husband give us the eye or that little indicator of, "how you doin"? We all know that look. But can I tell you, one of the best things you can do for your marriage is to be intimate with one another. When you let it be an afterthought and go too long without having sex, you start to feel disconnected. It is so important to keep that part of your marriage alive and healthy.

There is nothing to be ashamed of. In the garden of Eden, Adam and Eve had no shame. [The world didn't design sex to be a good thing. God did. Don't get it twisted. When it's done in the covenant of marriage, it's actually a command of God to bless a relationship.]

The bigger picture to this command, though, besides God giving them the green light to have sex in the context of marriage, is to be fruitful. To be fruitful there needs to be a seed. I believe God deposited "seeds" within every one of our children that we need to call out and develop. Every day we should be looking for ways to serve those seeds. It's in our homes we begin to recognize this, and put them in environments to flourish. It's been amazing to watch people who never realized they had things inside of them get around the right kinds of people with the right kinds of spirits and become strong, confident people.

At VIVE Culture, we believe that if people can get in environments where the seeds in them can be discovered and fertilized, then they can begin to produce the fruit in them that they were always meant to produce.

The fruit is the substance of the seed.

Serving your family isn't a small ministry. Teaching your kids how to love people right where they are at and to show kindness and be full of grace and wisdom is a big responsibility. My platform maybe wasn't standing up on a stage, but it didn't make it any less important. If anything, God was teaching me that this is the most important thing I will ever do. Why wait for the perfect position to come around when I could have missed out on speaking life into the people who were all around me? If you are in the workforce, serving the people around you and being a light in a dark place is the platform God gave you for this season.

We are always looking for what is ahead, but what are we doing with what is right in front of us? Are we wasting time wishing and hoping for something better, or starting to serve the people who are right around us now?

Bloom where you are planted.

In our church we repeat things over and over again—not because we run out of things to say, but because we know vision leaks. As humans we have short memories. That's why God often calls His people to remember certain things in the Bible:

 Remember who I am.
Remember who you are.
Remember what I've done for you.
Remember where I'm taking you.

Brian and I have a passion to believe in people. In fact, two of our favorite things you'll often hear us say is we have a passion to build the local church and desire to see people flourish within her. We love to raise and release leaders to lead, even before they think they are ready. There's not a season we have ever been in that we've ever felt ready for. And still, God sees something in us and pushes us to fulfill that.

I think so often people are going through the motions without realizing they are missing out on something greater for their life.

They are taking their kids to soccer practice.

They are putting in their forty hours at work.

They are paying the bills.

And all of a sudden they come into an environment of worship, or they get around other moms who actually enjoy motherhood, or they see what a healthy family looks like and they get a vision for their life—and something in their heart is stirred.

I want to encourage you to get around other women that not only stir your passions but fan the flame.

CHARACTER TRUMPS TALENT

I remember back when we were working in youth ministry there was this one student who was such a great kid. He wasn't really connected but he was always hanging around Brian and the band. So Brian decided to have him start playing drums. To be honest, he could keep a beat but it was nothing amazing. In fact, Brian would come home and tell me that there are other drummers in the youth ministry actually better than him playing in bands. But you have to know my husband. He's not impressed with talent.

Some leaders always look for the talented people around them to build their own credibility. They hire the person from the biggest church, or who seems to have the most talent. That's not Brian.

Brian will take character over talent any day of the week. You can teach talent. You can't teach character. Even though there may have been other drummers more talented, Brian saw something special in this teenager. One Wednesday night Brian found out that he was learning the acoustic guitar. So what does Brian do? He threw him on the mic to lead worship. This poor kid. My husband is intense. When he believes in someone he is relentless. Brian wouldn't just throw anyone on the mic. There were people in theater productions who wanted to be on the mic that Brian knew weren't ready for the mic.

We are all about developing your spirit so the light in you is greater than the lights on you. Someone once said, "If you aren't careful, your talent will take you where your character can't keep you." This student may not have been the most talented, but he saw seeds in this student that this student didn't even see in himself.

This young man kept trying to quit and talk Brian out of using him. Brian didn't give up on him. Eventually, this student bought his own acoustic guitar, Brian started to give him lessons, and eventually this student started leading worship every week alongside Brian.

Eventually, Brian let him lead on his own. After all these years, this young man went on to get married, have three young kids, and become a worship pastor who is now a lead pastor of his own church.

We are so proud of this young man leading his church and family in a great way. In fact, his church helped support VIVE when we launched. God is so good!

The greatest platform we have to develop those seeds, however, is inside of our homes in our own kids.

It all started with a seed. It started with servanthood.

YOUR SELF-WORTH WILL IMPACT HOW YOU SERVE

Let's not sugar-coat it. Being a wife is hard. Parenting is hard. Life is hard. Being a woman in today's day and age is hard. Ladies, we can't turn on the TV without seeing women with zero cellulite on their bodies and everything all nice and perky.

I see these women at the pool with perfect bodies and I'm like, "You push six humans out of your body and see if you still look like that."

I know. I still need Jesus.

The self-worth battles women go through are intense. I don't know one woman that can't tell you immediately what they don't like about their appearance. We compare ourselves with everyone around us. *If I only had that kind of skin . . . or that body . . . or that type of hair.* Can I just tell you, God doesn't make mistakes!

He made you perfect and He looks at you and knows you by name and knows all the battles you face and insecurities that you struggle with. He knows our failures and those ugly days. And He still is madly in love with us and wants to pursue a relationship with us. If we could only see ourselves through our Father's eyes!

There are some days where everything is falling into place and everyone is happy, and then some where I lay down at night and think of all the things I missed or am messing up, and all of it starts to feel overwhelming. It's easy to look at other people's life and become envious or dream of wanting more.

But what if we embraced those mundane things? It's in those unseen places that God builds the character within us needed to care for the vision He has for us. It's about faithfulness.

His master replied, "Well done, good and faithful servant! You have been faithful with a few things; I will put you in charge of many things. Come and share your master's happiness!"

(Matthew 25:23)

The not-so-glamorous days are actually launching pads toward fulfilling the calling in our lives. Embrace the waiting period and learn what God is teaching you through it. You know those people that seem to have it all together? Those who never seemed phased? They always seem happy and they always look perfect. Their house is perfect, and they have the most perfect family.

We all get so caught up in what social media tells us about certain people, and their "highlight reel"—and then the trap of comparison starts to creep in. You start to become discontent with what you have and start to feel lonely or not good enough.

Here's the thing . . . everyone goes through stuff.

No one is posting on social media when their kid is having a complete melt down and they are screaming at them to get their shoes on and get in the car. We can get so caught up in other people's life that we end up missing out on what God has for our own. We start comparing what we don't have and are never content with what we *do* have.

It's such a dangerous and slippery slope and if we aren't careful, we get so fixated on other people that we completely miss the calling God has for us. For me, I know my greatest calling is to be a wife and mother. That is the biggest platform I could ever have: to raise these kids to know their worth and to know what they were created for.

The mundane of motherhood, day-in and day-out stuff, is not glamorous. You don't get a promotion or a raise. Sometimes you wonder if what you are doing or saying is getting through, but staying faithful and finding the joy in it is what will get you though. Don't go through it alone. We were never meant to do life alone—just like Ruth wasn't going to let Naomi walk through life alone; they needed each other.

When you are in the early stages of motherhood, you can feel so alone, or that you are the only one feeling overwhelmed.

You aren't!

Don't let the enemy whisper lies in your ear.

You need girls around you who will fight with you and for you. If it's one person or a group, have your go-to people who can lift you up, and that you can lift up in return. Get around other ladies that have a vision for their family. Get around women that have a vision for their city and serve with them. Being around visionaries will impact how you serve.

When we change our mindset, it changes our perspective and how we handle life. Yes, we all have bad days and sometimes it is okay not to be okay, but it is not okay to stay there. Don't let the enemy dwell and live in that place of discontentment, bitterness, or loneliness. God has so much more for you than that.

IN NEED OF DAILY GRACE

I have to be honest. I never thought I would homeschool. It just wasn't for me. I didn't wear a denim jean dress or a bun in my hair. I wasn't patient enough. Growing up, homeschool kids were a little weird, and really, how was I to be able to teach my kids? I can't even remember what I learned at their age. Apparently, God had other plans. The only reason I decided to homeschool my oldest daughter was because I found out that kindergarten was all day.

All day!

What? My baby. My firstborn. I wasn't ready for her to be away from me for that long. I know some moms are thinking, "That's a mini-vacation to get stuff done." I just wasn't ready. My intention was to do one year and see how it went. Kaitlyn was the ideal first student. She caught on fast to things, she was reading chapter books by the end of kindergarten, and she did exactly what I told her to do.

So I thought to myself, "Hey, I got this. Let's do another year. Then came my second born, Makayla. Now I had Makayla in in kindergarten and Kaitlyn in first grade.

Lord, why? Just why? That year was tough! Makayla is my artsy child. She loves to cook, do hair, and get into everything she possibly can. She has such a creative mind. Doing things by the book isn't exactly how she is wired. I talked about Makayla earlier on how she was a completely different learner, and tested my patience. There were days that I would go in my room and just scream in a pillow.

My second born and I frequently cried, were frustrated, and felt insecure. This went on for three years. Most days I would think, "What am I doing? She would be better off learning from someone else." However, I knew God was having me still homeschool for some reason. It wasn't just for Makayla. It was also for me.

Toward the end of her second-grade year, we realized there was something more to it than that.

Makayla was dyslexic.

I had no idea! It made so much sense after everything I was seeing in her. It wasn't that she wasn't smart, or that she was being lazy. Her mind simply worked differently. Discovering that early on was one of the best things that could have happened for both of us.

[We didn't hide it from her. We didn't baby her. My husband tells our kids all the time, "This world doesn't owe you anything. Life isn't fair. And you will be let down. How are you going to handle it?" They probably can repeat that after all the times he's told them that.]

When we discovered what she had, it changed my entire way of teaching her. A year after we found out, she was talking about how she just isn't very smart. So I sat her down and began to walk her through what Dyslexia was and showed her all the celebrities and successful people in our world that had it that went on to do amazing things. By the end of our talk, Makayla was so excited that she had it because she wanted to be famous.

That wasn't exactly what we were trying to convey. In fact, my oldest daughter was disappointed that she wasn't dyslexic because she wanted to be famous. She said, "Oh man. I wish I was dyslexic. Is there anyone cool that isn't dyslexic?"

Oh, sweet child of mine.

Makayla is one of the sweetest, most compassionate girls you will ever meet. She works so hard and has come such a long way. Now that we are teaching her in a way that her mind understands, it's amazing to see her start to come alive and really believe that she is smart and capable. Since we discovered her dyslexia, her spirit has completely changed toward school. When she reads a whole book, the smile on her face is priceless.

She was always smart. She just had to believe it for herself.

For so long I thought I was homeschooling because I didn't want to let go of my babies. Little did I know that it was to help me grow and instill confidence in me that I could do it, to push me to be faithful and diligent in the hard things. Paul spoke of this in his letter to the Corinthians:

> My grace is sufficient for you, for my power is made perfect in weakness. Therefore, I will boast all the more gladly about my weakness, so that Christ's power may rest on me.

(2 Corinthians 12: 9–10)

I cling to that verse every day. I was relying so much on myself to "fix" Makayla and failing in every sense of the word. I felt helpless and defeated because I was trying to do it on my own. I'm so grateful that God gives us a special grace in every season of our lives and restores and uses our weakness to rely on Him. I could not do anything that I do without Him. I am a mess without Him.

LEAVE THE MESS AND ENJOY THE JOURNEY

Oh the pressures we face now-a-days to have everything perfect! I'll admit that I love Pinterest. And don't get me started on Fixer Upper and my love for Joanna Gaines.

I talk with too many wives and mothers who have become so high strung because they are busy trying to keep everything perfect. Y'll, I have a never-ending pile of laundry, and bedrooms that sometimes look like we just got robbed.

I try to keep a clean house and I believe in teaching our kids responsibility. Don't get me wrong. However, there are times where you just have to leave the mess and enjoy your family. Give yourself permission to leave the dishes after dinner to have dance parties with your kids in the living room. Let your kids enjoy the home you live in instead of making them feel like they have to keep everything perfect. Some of you start to get anxiety just thinking of leaving a mess. Just don't put so much pressure on yourself to have everything always perfect and put together. It will be ok.

Ladies, it's so important to remember to enjoy the journey.

So many wives and mothers are always talking about someday. The joy is in the journey. The joy comes with whom you get to share life with as you raise your families together. Take one day at a time—sometimes one moment knowing that in your weakness He is strong, and He gives new mercies every morning. Thank you Jesus for that.

I absolutely love the team that my husband and I get to share life with. We have never led our ministries with an organization mindset, but rather with a family dynamic. We couldn't imagine doing ministry any other way than with people we love to be around. And all the time I poured into sowing and nurturing my home, nine years later, God is now opening up doors of dreams from years and years ago.

I am privileged to co-pastor VIVE Culture with my husband and lead a passionate, relational, life-giving church by pouring into people. We have added more kids, I still have young kids, and I still know my first priority is them. Honestly, I believe God was preparing my heart all those years for this season we are walking in.

I still battle many insecurities and doubts daily. The enemy would want nothing more than to see me believe the lies.

To feel defeated.

But thank God that greater is He that is in me than he that is in the world!

I want to leave you with this.

Speak life into your husbands. I cannot say this enough. You have no idea the pressures men face in today's culture. They may not say it, but they are feeling it. Society has painted a picture of men that they are useless and incapable of being a good dad or husband. Too many times when we get together and have our girls' nights we start taking shots at the expense of our husbands. Yes, I get it. Marriage is hard. It takes work, and it is a constant selfless act of thinking of the other person.

Our husbands do things that sometimes make us shake our heads. If anyone makes fun of himself, it's Brian. That's what I love about him. He takes our lives and becomes an open book to people and applies those successes, failures, and everything in-between to lead people to Jesus.

He'll be the first to admit that he can do some dumb stuff.

But even through the dumb stuff, I am crazy about him. I love him more now than the day I married him. Is our marriage perfect? Not even close. Do we get in arguments? Sometimes.

We have changed and grown so much from when we got married in 2005. Brian isn't the same person he was at twenty-four as he is at thirty-eight. I was not the same person at twenty-one that I am at thirty-four. We are learning how to grow old together. But one thing is certain: there is nothing I love more than being around my family. They can brighten my day with a sweet compliment, by telling bad knock-knock jokes around the table, or simply by running up and giving me the biggest hug. And the newborn stage. I just can't get enough of it. When they are babies, they have that look like you are the most amazing thing they've ever seen. Just one look and I want to give them whatever they want, every time.

Ladies, I want to encourage you that being a wife is one of the greatest things you are called to. I love being a mom, but I love being a wife even more. To share life with a man I respect and admire is the best thing I could ever imagine. There was a time when all I was wrapped up in was motherhood. I was only wrapped up in my kids, and forgetting to nurture and invest in my marriage. I would light up when I was with them—but then, when it was just Brian and me, I acted tired and worn out and took him for granted.

I'm so thankful for grace through the journey.

We are in a season where life is very busy with kids, whom we love, but I never want to forget to put my marriage first, and show our kids that.

They know that their dad and I are always there for them and love them with everything inside of us. But the best thing that Brian and I can do for our family and for our church is to have a healthy marriage and to show it. Not just tell people, but to actually tell each other how we feel about each other and to show it with our attention and how we prioritize one another. Laugh together. It is so good to laugh a lot and have fun with each other. It's good for the soul . . . and sometimes, our sanity.

There is a calling on your life as the woman of your home that is special and unique for you. There is something powerful about brave, confident, women of God who lead their homes. It's those women who, when they are having one of "those" days, don't go and hide but instead say, "Not today, devil. Not today."

Ladies, it's so important to recognize the season you are in so you don't wish away the moments in life. God may be trying to develop something in you to better lead your family.

You are amazing and made for greatness. Just know that.

6

serving when we feel let down

Did you ever dream of doing something as a kid that never worked out? I remember the first time I saw the music video Black or White on MTV by the great Michael Jackson. I was eleven years old when it first debuted and I had never seen anything like that in my life. He had so much confidence and charisma. I wanted to be that type of rock star who could perform in front of millions of screaming fans. There was something so magnetic about the energy of the song that made me want to be him.

In fact, I'm embarrassed to admit that I was insanely jealous of Macaulay Culkin in that video. I wanted to trade lives with him. I loved his big red clothes and the massive bling around his neck. I memorized his rap and emulated him in the mirror. I didn't really believe I could be Michael Jackson until my mom saw me dancing in the mirror one day and said, "Wow you could really be a great dancer, son." I took it as a sign from heaven. This was what I was made to do.

I put extra time into working on my hip motions, popping my hands, and biting my lip a certain way. I thought my moves were on point. That was until I went to my first middle school dance in sixth grade.

I was so excited. It was my first school dance. This was going to be the beginning of the rest of my life—some record label guy who was scouting at middle school dances might discover my amazing talent. This was my chance to make the ladies go crazy and put them on notice. I remember walking into my first school dance wearing baggy pants and a purple silk shirt.

My hair was carefully slicked to the side with a half a tube of LA Gear hair gel to cement it in place. I had my Jordache sneakers polished with soap and water and I was ready to light up the dance floor. I had a little extra swag in my walk that evening. I walked in with my boys, put on some cherry chap stick, popped in a breath mint, and headed out to that dance floor.

Once I stepped out onto the dance floor and got around other students, I realized I couldn't dance to save my life. It was awful. I was awful.

I was like Albert in the movie Hitch. Looking back, I wish I would have shown someone my moves before I tested them out in public. I wish I had a Hitch in my life back then to love me enough to say, "Brian, just stick with the two step. Elbows six inches from the waste at a ninety-degree angle."

I needed someone to tell me not to bite my lips when I danced. It was a total disaster.

All I kept thinking as I was making a fool of myself was: my mom lied to me. Once I realized I couldn't dance, my dreams of becoming a dance icon were shattered.

I think that was the first time I could remember feeling like my dreams were squashed. As adults we look back at memories like that and just laugh, but as a kid, you believe anything is possible. I don't blame my mom at all. Parents are supposed to lie to their kids and tell them they can do the impossible.

You know what I'm talking about. Every parent has told their child that they did wonderful in the school play, even though they were the only one standing there digging out their wedgie. As a parent, you are supposed to clap for the plays they perform in the living room even though it's the worst thing you've ever seen in your life. When your kid shows you a picture they drew, and they drew on every part of the paper except for inside the lines, you don't tell them they should never attempt to color again.

No! You lie to them and tell them how creative their mind is and you put it on the fridge to scare guests when they come over.

I understand this now as a parent. I didn't back then. As a kid, you begin to dream of things that are beyond what is really possible to achieve. When I was a kid, there was no YouTube to size up your skills against the rest of the world. You just had your imagination. I thought I could be Michael Jackson until I saw other students who could actually dance. It was something so small but I still can remember that feeling of being let down.

What happens though, when it's a dream we feel like we've been given from God? Many of us can't imagine it playing out any other way than with a happy ending.

"If it's from God, then it'll work out perfectly," we tell ourselves.

There was a teenager in the book of Genesis that was a dreamer. His dreams were massive. When other people dreamed of bigger lots of land, or selling more cattle, this young man had dreams of ruling a nation. His name was Joseph. Joseph was born to Jacob and Rachel, the couple we talked about a few chapters ago. Jacob deeply loved Joseph.

Jacob lived in the land where his father had stayed, the land of Canaan.

This is the account of Jacob's family line. Joseph, a young man of seventeen, was tending the flocks with his brothers—the sons of Bilhah and the sons of Zilpah, his father's wives—and Joseph brought his father a bad report about them:

Now Israel loved Joseph more than any of his other sons, because he had been born to him in his old age; and he made an ornate robe for him. When his brothers saw that their father loved him more than any of them, they hated him and could not speak a kind word to him.

Joseph had a dream, and when he told it to his brothers, they hated him all the more.

(Genesis 37:1–5)

Joseph was like any typical teenager—cocky, overly confident, and constantly trying to annoy his siblings. Here Joseph, similar to David, was serving his house in the fields. However, unlike David, Joseph had a different spirit about him. He knew he was the favorite child. He was the kid that would wait for you to do something wrong so he could run to mom and dad and tattletale.

Joseph was *that* teenager. He was spoiled and he knew it. He was always trying to get his brothers in trouble. That type of spirit bred so much envy and hatred in the hearts of his brothers. If we are being honest, can you really blame them for hating Joseph? As an older brother, I can say as much as I love my brothers now, there were times growing up when I just wanted to push their heads through a wall.

Joseph had that type of gift. He could make you so angry just by running to dad and snitching on you. One night Joseph had a dream—and it was a big dream. As you get older you learn to protect the dreams God gives you, because any time you get a God-sized dream you can be sure that dream killers will be waiting to discredit anything you believe you are called to do.

When God spoke to Alicia and me that we would lead our own church someday, we didn't tell a soul. We kept it in our hearts until it was time to do something with it. Why? We knew people would try and talk us out of it. We knew that people who live to put in their thirty years, build their 401K, and retire on a beach can't comprehend a life other than making the most money they can. So we chose to protect this dream God gave us.

That comes with maturity. Not everything God speaks to your heart is for social media or the world to know.

Joseph was seventeen years old. He had experienced so much grief and ridicule from his older brothers that this was his time to elevate himself. This was his time to show his brothers that he was somebody. Joseph went on to tell his brothers his dream and, knowing what we know about Joseph, I imagine he didn't quite tell it in the humblest way.

He said to them, "Listen to this dream I had: We were binding sheaves of grain out in the field when suddenly my sheaf rose and stood upright, while your sheaves gathered around mine and bowed down to it." His brothers said to him, "Do you intend to reign over us? Will you actually rule us?" And they hated him all the more because of his dream and what he had said.

(Genesis 37:6–8)

Joseph told his brothers his dream of the sheaves bowing down to him, likely smiling from ear-to-ear. But to be fair, let's give Joseph the benefit of the doubt for a moment. Let's just say he had a teenage moment and didn't think before he spoke. Imagine with me for a moment he was a typical teenager and didn't think this one through.

We can understand that. We've all been there. As adults, we are still there, aren't we? We all have moments where we don't think before we speak and wish we could take what we said back. Hopefully, we learn from our mistakes. We get it. We all have bad moments. Joseph shared his dream, and then realized the reaction wasn't quite what he was expecting and had a chance to make an adjustment.

You would think he would have sensed the moment and thought, "You know what? Next time I'll just keep these dreams to myself."

I can't prove this, but maybe Joseph actually liked to get a rise out of his brothers because he knew Jacob would protect him. Don't you hate that about your little brother or sister? Maybe Joseph was that annoying because he wanted to make his brothers so mad they would react, because he knew he could run to daddy.

When I was growing up, I hated that my little brother could make me so mad at times that I would react, ending up in trouble, while he was allowed to go out and play with his friends. I would be fuming in my room while I waited for my punishment, listening to him play outside. Don't get me wrong. My little brother is awesome. He was a great kid and most of the time we had fun together.

However, he was raised differently than my older brother and me. He was allowed to get away with things we never were allowed to get away with. Joseph should have learned his lesson. But like many of us, he didn't. Then, he had another dream, and he told it to his brothers:

> "Listen," he said, "I had another dream, and this time the sun and moon and eleven stars were bowing down to me."
>
> When he told his father as well as his brothers, his father rebuked him and said, "What is this dream you had? Will your mother and I and your brothers actually come and bow down to the ground before you?" His brothers were jealous of him, but his father kept the matter in mind.
>
> (Genesis 37:9–11)

Joseph not only told his brothers, but this time he told his own father his dream. Joseph, Joseph, Joseph. You never bite the hand that feeds you. You don't insult the only person on the planet who is in your corner. It's not shocking that the second time around didn't go quite as planned, either.

Joseph is like you or me. When we receive a God-sized dream, we expect everything to work out smoothly. Usually, though, there is a process that God must take us through. Joseph thought the dream was about people serving him. He totally missed that the dream was actually his call to serve others. Joseph didn't realize that the dream wasn't about him at all. The dream was all about God saving His people.

> So Joseph went after his brothers and found them near Dothan. But they saw him in the distance, and before he reached them, they plotted to kill him. "Here comes that dreamer!" they said to each other. "Come now, let's kill him and throw him into one of these cisterns and say that a ferocious animal devoured him. Then we'll see what comes of his dreams."
>
> When Reuben heard this, he tried to rescue him from their hands. "Let's not take his life," he said. "Don't shed any blood. Throw him

into this cistern here in the wilderness, but don't lay a hand on him." Reuben said this to rescue him from them and take him back to his father.

So when Joseph came to his brothers, they stripped him of his robe—the ornate robe he was wearing—and they took him and threw him into the cistern. The cistern was empty; there was no water in it.

(Genesis 37:17–24)

Here was the beginning of the end of Joseph's dream. You will notice a common theme throughout the Bible. The spirit of envy is ruthless in a human heart. Some people can't stand to see your elevation. Some people just can't stand to see your success. They can't stand when you move into your dream home or you are offered the big promotion at work.

Envy is ruthless and Joseph's brothers were full of it. They couldn't get past their own hatred for Joseph, and Joseph couldn't move past his pride to love his brothers. Joseph was serving in the fields out of duty, but God needed him to learn what it really meant to serve with a spirit of honor and humility. Joseph had to learn what it really meant to serve so he could be the type of leader that would eventually be used to save the very people trying to kill him.

Joseph's life changed in one moment. When you continue to read the story we learn that Joseph lost everything he loved. Not only was he stripped of his identity when they stripped him of his robe, but he lost his family and security as well.

I am sure many of you can relate to Joseph. Maybe you had a dream in your heart that you were going to have a big family and then one day you realized you were unable to conceive. Maybe you were living the American dream and one day got a call from the doctor's office that you had terminal brain cancer. Maybe one day you had a dream to be in ministry and in a moment's time a close family member or friend took away your innocence and you were left feeling ashamed, alone, and abandoned.

Joseph went through a spiritual boot camp to really learn what it would mean to serve no matter where you find yourself. In the middle of all of that, you will notice something profound that we can hold on to in our own lives.

The Lord was with Joseph so that he prospered, and he lived in the house of his Egyptian master.

(Genesis 39:2)

A consistent theme in Joseph's life was that the Lord was with him. Even when life didn't make sense, Joseph prospered. When he was in the pit, the Lord was with Joseph. When he was elevated to the palace, the Lord was with Joseph. When he was sent to prison for being falsely accused, the Lord was with Joseph.

The Lord was doing something in Joseph's heart with every step of Joseph's journey. Even the moments when Joseph was angry and questioning God's will, the Lord was with him. When we were first introduced to Joseph, he was all about himself. He hadn't learned yet that God was all about God, and every God-sized dream is about serving people and leading them to experience freedom. Every dream you and I have, if it's a God-sized dream, will be all about God using us to lead people toward His heart.

In every God-sized dream we have, God is the lead story—not us. Sometimes the path to move us toward our destiny involves being pushed out of our comfort zones and into an unfamiliar place where we are forced to be fully dependent on Him.

For Americans, that isn't a popular place to be. We do everything we can to structure our lives to be as comfortable as possible.

The more I journey with people and hear about the struggles others are walking through the more I realize this idea of serving through disappointment has become harder and harder to embrace in our Western world. What do you do when you feel let down or betrayed? Quit? Do you go back to your old way of living? Are you filled with so much envy and that you become bitter at anyone moving forward in life? It's one thing to feel abandoned when you have been let down by friends or a family member. It's a whole other feeling when you feel like God has let you down.

The story of Joseph is a remarkable one.

Joseph even had to learn to serve leaders that believed completely different than he did. Think about that for a moment. In our day and age, Joseph would have been on the complete other side of the political spectrum as his leader over him. And still, he honored him. And yes, he found favor with his leaders because he chose to serve.

God ended up fulfilling His purpose for Joseph. The old Joseph still popped up at times, but in the end, God fulfilled His purpose of saving His people just like He had revealed to Joseph in the dream when he was a teenager.

Joseph had to go through the school of hard knocks to understand that if he wanted to be used in a great way, the pathway came through servanthood. Those are hard lessons to learn.

I NEVER ASKED FOR THIS

When I was a senior in high school I was introduced to this adult Christian leader who served students in our city. I'll call him Bill to protect his identity. Bill seemed to have a great spirit and as we began to build a relationship I shared with him a need I saw for teenagers my age who were about to graduate to grow in their faith.

At the time, there was nothing in my area for graduating students to grow in their relationship with Jesus. I began to share my heart with him and we decided that we would start a Bible study in his house and he convinced me to lead it. I was so scared because I had never done anything like that.

I wasn't looking to lead anything. I just wanted to provide something for students to grow in their relationship with Jesus and connect with one another. I was perfectly happy just sitting in the background and being part of the group. However, Bill insisted I lead my own peers.

The first night that we met we had two people show up—one other student, and me. It wasn't quite the vision I had in mind. However, we kept it going. I didn't have a vision for it to be anything because I had never done anything like this before. In fact, the only reason I learned to play the guitar was to lead worship at that Bible study. We would worship, I would stumble through a devotion that I led, and then we would hang out together.

I remember doing a whole devotion and at the end of it I realized I was talking about the wrong character in the Bible. Lord have mercy! God should have given up on me right then. I didn't know it at the time, but God was building me in those early days to lead my own church someday. I graduated high school and over the next six months, God would begin to lead adult leaders to our group as we began to build a great community.

Bill's street was lined up with cars from one block to the next each week from people coming to this Bible study. His house was packed wall-to-wall, from the living room on back, with bodies and people singing as loud as they could in worship. I get goose bumps even now just thinking about it. The atmosphere of worship in that place was something so special.

As time went on, the students and leaders who gathered each week began to get a bigger vision that we could reach even more college students in our area. We quickly began to outgrow Bill's home and tension began to stir inside Bill's heart. He wanted it to stay small and wanted to have complete control over it.

He wasn't happy at all with the direction it was headed.

We knew trouble was coming when Bill began to hijack the devotions and go on and on, and lose everyone. We tried to talk to him about it, but the more we confronted him, the worse the situation became. Let's just say there wasn't a healthy feedback culture with him.

It was obvious a change needed to happen. All of our leaders felt it. We just didn't know what to do.

So I met with one of our adult leaders that I trusted and shared with her that I took it upon myself to find a new location to meet. God opened a door and we found a church that would allow us to use their facility for free on Thursday evenings. We could have a full band for worship and use anything we wanted. I knew I had to meet with Bill and let him know we would be relocating and pursuing the vision we had to reach more college students.

I will never forget the phone conversation we had when I stepped out from under his covering. Initially, the plan was for us meet in person with one of our adult leaders to share our heart and get his blessing. I didn't need his blessing. As an eighteen-year-old, I didn't even want it. I didn't even want to meet with him. It got so bad that I just wanted to be done with him. The way he treated his family and how he treated others caused me to lose all respect for him.

However, I received wise counsel to honor the process even though I no longer respected Bill. Honor had nothing to do with how little I respected this man. Honor is really a heart issue. Those leaders who counseled my young heart were absolutely right. To be fair, Bill was the reason we started this Bible study in the first place. It would have never started if he didn't push me to rally students together. So it was only right that I thanked him for the opportunity that he provided for us and let him know how much we appreciated that he opened up his home.

I was eighteen years old, working at In-N-Out Burger, going to Jr. College, and was leading my first growing ministry.

The day we were supposed to meet in person, I got a phone call from this man saying that he changed his mind and he didn't want anyone to be at the meeting with us. He wanted it to just be him, his wife, and myself. I may have been young, but I wasn't stupid.

I have seen enough to know that Bill was temperamental to say the least and used that frequently to intimidate people. I was young but I stood my ground. I insisted that I would not meet with him without one of our adult leaders, for accountability. I'll never forget what this man said to me. Remember, this is a guy with whom I shared my life with. I was always around his family. He would encourage me, speak life into me, and told me that God was going to use me in a great way. I guess that meant only if I did things his way.

He said plenty on the phone that day. He was not a man of few words. But I can never forget one specific thing he said to me. He was so angry that I wouldn't meet with him alone, without any other leaders present, and finally said: "Don't bother coming over. You are a cocky, arrogant young man and you are going to fail. As far as I'm concerned, we are through and I'm going to start my own Bible study with a group of students without you."

That was that. And he did. He took some of students in our group and they did their own Bible study.

That caused a huge split with a group of us who were close. You would think since it was a college-led ministry that Bill would be secure enough to cheer us on even if he didn't agree with how we were doing it. Sadly, that wasn't the case. It was a mess.

I hung up the phone and was crushed. Of course, when you are eighteen you think you have to be invincible so you try and fake your way through it. That's never a good idea. I didn't know any better back then.

[We moved forward with what we were feeling God was doing in us and started to meet in another location. Our small group of people began to serve a college ministry of over 150 college students every Thursday night. It never was intended to be that, but there was such a spirit of worship in that place that people leaned into the Word when it was preached and had a passion to do something great with their lives.]

The Bible study that Bill started didn't last long. I wish I had been mature enough to handle it well. I wasn't. I was happy to hear that it failed. I'm not sure what happened, but it fizzled out.

My prayers started to sound like this: "Forget him. I don't respect him, I never want to be like him, and I don't ever want to talk to him again."

I know, that doesn't sound very spiritual, but it was a very raw, immature conversation I had with God as a young man. As our ministry grew, my heart was growing harder each week that passed. I wasn't ready to lead. God had to work on my heart. I just wasn't ready to let Him.

Bill will never know this, but that was one of the most hurtful things I experienced as a young man just starting out in ministry. I rarely cry, but one night driving home after we had a record-breaking attendance of over 165 people at a service, I broke down. I had too much anger in my heart. I told God I never asked for this ministry or this calling. I never asked for this dream.

Why me?

All I wanted to do was serve and it ended up costing me friendships, and for a season, tarnished my reputation with people.

Rumors spread about what happened between Bill and me and how we were parting ways, and I never had a chance to defend myself. Everything that was said happened over a phone call. I wanted to meet in person, for accountability. That opportunity never happened; Bill refused to meet face to face.

To be honest, no matter what I said, would it have really mattered? The lines were drawn and there was nothing I could do to change it. I didn't know this then, but God was up to something.

I remember God softly speaking to my heart reminding me that He promised that He would fulfill His dreams for me. He never promised that He would fulfill my dreams for myself.

That was a game changer. Throughout the years by God's grace I have matured. I have forgiven this man, and even believe the best for him and his family. We've all said things we wish we could take back. I know I have. But God used that to continue to build in me what He was preparing for me.

I don't know where Bill is anymore and it doesn't really matter to be honest. All I know is that difficult season wasn't about him, or me for that matter. What the enemy intended for evil God was intending to use for good.

When we feel like a dream has died, it's easy to blame God instead of running toward Him. No one knew this more than this Shunammite woman in 2 Kings.

LET HOPE RISE

Hope is a powerful thing.

The great thing about hope is that it doesn't have an expiration date.

I believe miracles happen when we continue to serving and remain faithful.

There is an amazing story of a Shunammite woman in the Bible. In fact, this woman's name is never revealed. What we do know about her is that her pathway for the miracle she experienced came through serving others. She didn't just serve to get a task done. This woman served to bless people.

Sometimes people make their calling too complicated. What is our purpose when we wake up?

To be a blessing and serve people. It's amazing what opportunities open up for us when we spend our lives serving others.

Serving paved the way for this woman to have one of her biggest dreams answered. I would guess that if she didn't serve well, she would never have had the opportunity she was given.

Something powerful happens when we serve with no strings attached. This woman that we are going to look at wasn't expecting anything in return. She was just serving. I love surrounding myself with those types of spirits—people who see a need and find ways to get it done. No ask is too big and no task is too small.]

> Now it happened one day that Elisha went to Shunem, where there was a notable woman, and she persuaded him to eat some food. So it was, as often as he passed by, he would turn in there to eat some food. And she said to her husband, "Look now, I know that this is a holy man of God, who passes by us regularly. Please, let us make a small upper room on the wall; and let us put a bed for him there, and a table and a chair and a lampstand; so it will be, whenever he comes to us, he can turn in there." And it happened one day that he came there, and he turned in to the upper room and lay down there.

> (2 Kings 4:8–10 NKJV)

Elisha crossed paths with a notable woman. It's important that we understand that she wasn't just any woman. She was wealthy and influential. We don't even know how she came to faith, but we do know that she had spiritual character. She was living a comfortable lifestyle. She was an influential woman who wasn't entitled. She was a real leader who led through servanthood. Apparently, Elisha enjoyed being around this family so much that he continued to come back when he was in town.

[There are some people in life that you meet that you connect with and say, "They are the type of family I want to be around. There is something about their spirit, the way they parent, and the way they do life together that is magnetic."]

I call them lifers. Lifers are people you meet that you would love to stay around the rest of your life. They aren't common friendships. They aren't common people. When you meet that person or that couple, you hold on to them. *+ LUKE + HEATHER   * J + KELLY   * JARED + SAM   * KEION + MANNY

That was the home environment this notable woman created.

Not only did this woman carry a servant's heart, but she also knew what it meant to honor her leaders. [When someone carries a spirit of servanthood mixed with a spirit of honor, they go above and beyond to make sure their leaders are cared for.] That is a powerful combination that opens up the doors for God to perform miracles for us. When we serve other people's dreams, God always takes care of our dreams, too.

She didn't make Elisha feel like he was an inconvenience. [Some people will do a task for you but complain the whole time, reminding you how they went out of their way to help you. That defeats the whole point of blessing someone. If you are going to serve and honor someone, make that person feel like it was a privilege.]

The team I get to serve with has a saying around the office. We say, "It's my pleasure." Why? Because it really is. It's our pleasure to serve one another. It is our privilege to serve His Church in our city. When we take care of one another, we aren't trying to make them feel guilty for how much it costs us. No. We want people to feel loved and valued.

2.) [It's about cause over comfort. It's amazing the extent that people will go to help build something when they carry a "cause over comfort" spirit. No task is too big and no ask is too great.]

3.) [This woman didn't grow annoyed and say she didn't have a big enough house or didn't make enough money to host Elisha. She used what she had to do something. She wanted to serve. She wanted to be proactive. You don't need a ministry to start serving. You don't need a building to start impacting people. You don't need a social media account to make a difference in someone's life. Just use what you have and start serving.]

Then he said to Gehazi his servant, "Call this Shunammite woman." When he had called her, she stood before him. And he said to him, "Say now to her, 'Look, you have been concerned for us with all this care. What can I do for you?'"

(2 Kings 4:12–13a NKJV)

In other words, "This Shunammite woman has served us well and put everyone else's needs above her own." When you serve with everything you have, people take notice. Elisha was saying, "You blessed us so much that now we want to bless you." Isn't that the truth? When someone is a blessing to you or your family, you want to bless them in return.

"Do you want me to speak on your behalf to the king or to the commander of the army?" She answered, "I dwell among my own people."

(2 Kings 4:13b NKJV)

Let me put this in modern terminology: she was implying that she had a great family. She was taken care of. She was happy. She wasn't doing it for any angle. She wasn't serving with a hidden agenda to get promoted.

So he said, "What then is to be done for her?" And Gehazi answered, "Actually, she has no son, and her husband is old."

(2 Kings 4:14 NKJV)

I think it's amazing that Elisha's servant noticed little details like this. When Gehazi was asked what could be done he didn't answer, "I don't know. What do you think?" Gehazi was attentive and aware. I could see him being around Elisha long enough to know how he thinks and what he looks for in others. I can imagine he was asked the question before on how they could serve people.

I have team members who have been around me so long that they know what I value and how I think so we can duplicate that heart and spirit in others. Great team members always understand your heart and are looking for ways to take ownership. Most likely this notable woman carried this pain of not being able to have a child. No matter how hard she tried to hide it, I'm sure Gehazi saw it on her face when she looked around her community and saw everyone having family days. Can you imagine how she felt when she saw other people watching their kids kicking rocks in the dirt and she didn't get to experience that same joy?

We all know that look—when someone puts on a happy face, but clearly there is a look of loss. Of course the Shunammite woman learned how live without a family and not think about it anymore; she had probably settled within her heart that a family wasn't in the cards for her:

> So he said, "Call her." When he had called her, she stood in the doorway. Then he said, "About this time next year you shall embrace a son." And she said, "No, my lord. Man of God, do not lie to your maidservant!"
>
> (2 Kings 4:15–16 NKJV)

The Shunammite woman was basically saying, "Stop trying to get my hopes up because I believed, prayed, and worshiped for a baby but it hasn't happened yet. If God wanted me to have a son, He would have allowed me to have one. I got my hopes up and my dreams were shattered. Stop it!"

Verse 17 is so encouraging because it says, "Because of her great faith..."

No, I'm just playing. It doesn't say that. That would be the churchy thing to say, right? Because they sang so loudly, God blessed them. Because they knew every Bible verse at Bible camp, God blessed them. Sometimes God even blesses us despite us. Aren't you thankful for that? God is a good Father and even when we lack faith and struggle through doubt and questions, He is trying to find ways to bless us. This woman of great character still was human and had doubts and God allowed space for that. God's grace is just amazing to me. Verse 17 actually says this:

But the woman conceived, and bore a son when the appointed time had come, of which Elisha had told her. And the child grew. Now it happened one day that he went out to his father, to the reapers. And he said to his father, "My head, my head!" So he said to his servant, "Carry him to his mother."

(2 Kings 4:17–19 NKJV)

This is perfect. Dads, this should encourage you. This is confirmation that no matter what century it is, men will be men.

This notable woman had a son and what is interesting about this story is we aren't even given the son's name either. We have a notable woman and her son. That's all we know. Her dream came true. She got to raise her son and experience all the blessings of motherhood as she watched him grow up. Apparently one day he got a horrible headache.

Most dads who read that verse can identify with this boy's father. I don't know any dad in the world who would tell a son complaining about a headache, "You poor thing. Come on my lap and let me hold you."

What are dads known for saying?

"Go see your mother!"

That's what we do.

There are some things we are wired for and other things we are not.

My kids know I love them with every fiber of my being. However, when they are hurt or sick, I'm the last person they run to. I usually say, "You'll be fine. Just pretend like it doesn't hurt and the pain will go away."

When my kids fall, my first reaction is to say, "You cool? You might not want to do that again or it'll hurt." I know, I admit, I'm not the most sensitive man on the planet.

When he had taken him and brought him to his mother, he sat on her knees till noon, and then died.

(2 Kings 4:20 NKJV)

This is so tragic. What we learned was it wasn't just a migraine headache.

Something unexpected happened that day that changed everything for this family. This wasn't how it was supposed to end. This boy was a dream-come-true. This boy was a gift from God. This young man was supposed to be a fulfilled promise. How could this happen? I can't imagine the pain of having to watch your kid die in your arms. I imagine, like any parent in that moment, the woman probably felt like all the oxygen left her body and she couldn't breathe because her heart hurt so badly. I imagine, like any parent, she wanted to die with her son. In one second, her dream was gone.

Many people read that story and ache for the mother, as they should. However, when I read that story and my heart ached for the father as well. As the head of your home, you can't fix that type of pain. There is not enough money in the world that can replace losing one of your kids.

I can't imagine the weeping that was happening in that home. This woman could have blamed God. But there was a fight inside of this woman for the dreams God placed in her. Scripture next says:

> And she went up and laid him on the bed of the man of God, shut the door upon him, and went out. Then she called to her husband, and said, "Please send me one of the young men and one of the donkeys, that I may run to the man of God and come back."
>
> (2 Kings 4:21–22 NKJV)

Now, men, have you ever had one of those moments where you sense your woman has flipped a switch and she is temporarily insane? Let's admit it; we can be clueless at times. However, we never miss a clue when we sense that a woman is about to go off. We are pre-wired to sense when freak-out mode is in full effect:

> So he said, "Why are you going to him today? It is neither the New Moon nor the Sabbath." And she said, "It is well."
>
> (2 Kings 4:23 NKJV)

Let's put her response in terms we can understand. This woman was saying, "Honey, I love you. But if you don't get out of my way or if you ask me one more question you may not live long enough to ask a second one." She was giving him a heads up that if he didn't find her a donkey he could kiss sleeping with her for the rest of the week goodbye.

> And so she departed, and went to the man of God at Mount Carmel. So it was, when the man of God saw her afar off, that he said to his servant Gehazi, "Look, the Shunammite woman! Please run now to meet her, and say to her, 'Is it well with you? Is it well with your husband? Is it well with the child?'" And she answered, "It is well."
>
> (2 Kings 4:25–26 NKJV)

Now, at first you would think she was lying to his face. Of course things weren't "well." Her son had just died and her dreams were shattered. It was not fine. Her life was in ruins. She was carrying pain in her heart that no parent should ever have to carry. Why in the world did she say, "It is well," when she knew her life was in pieces?

Because sometimes you have to confess over your life, even though it's not all right, that it's going to be all right. She was preaching to her own soul that it felt like it was hopeless right now, but was going to be okay:

> Now when she came to the man of God at the hill, she caught him by the feet, but Gehazi came near to push her away. But the man of God said, "Let her alone; for her soul is in deep distress, and the Lord has hidden it from me, and has not told me." So she said, "Did I ask a son of my lord? Did I not say, 'Do not deceive me'?" I didn't even ask you for this.
>
> (2 Kings 4:27–28 NKJV)

This woman said what many of us say to God when a dream is lost: "I never asked for this. This is Your fault."

God, I told You I was just fine without getting my hopes up.
I told You I didn't want to step out and take a chance on that relationship.
I told You if I tried to ask for forgiveness from that person who abused me that it would turn around on me.
I was doing just fine without getting a vision for my life.
I was comfortable making a living, minding my own business, and living the American dream.
God, I trusted You.

Then he said to Gehazi, "Get yourself ready, and take my staff in your hand, and be on your way. If you meet anyone, do not greet him; and if anyone greets you, do not answer him; but lay my staff on the face of the child." And the mother of the child said, "As the LORD lives, and as your soul lives, I will not leave you."

(2 Kings 4:29–30 NKJV)

I like this mother. She reminds me of an Italian mother. She has some spice to her personality. This woman was like, "A staff? No, no, no Mr. Elisha. A stick won't fix this one. I am not leaving this place without you. If you need me to pack your bags and load up your donkey for you, I will. But you are coming back with me if I have to tie you to my donkey and carry you back myself."

That's what an Italian mom would say.

Obviously I'm paraphrasing, but that's what this mother is thinking. She didn't want Elisha's stick. She wanted Elisha to fix the situation. She thought the promise came through Elisha. Elisha was just the messenger. It was really God that provided her a son.

He could have used the phrase, "Don't shoot the messenger."

Elisha was a smart man, though. He sensed that this mother was about to go nuclear on him if he didn't comply. This mother was stubborn enough to fight for her dream.

> Now Gehazi went on ahead of them, and laid the staff on the face of the child; but there was neither voice nor hearing. Therefore, he went back to meet him, and told him, saying, "The child has not awakened." When Elisha came into the house, there was the child, lying dead on his bed. He went in therefore, shut the door behind the two of them, and prayed to the Lord.

> (2 Kings 4:31–33 NKJV)

The staff didn't work. I'm sure this woman was so glad she didn't settle for the stick but instead fought hard enough to compel Elisha to come with her.

I love this story because Elisha was willing to go above and beyond for this woman who went above and beyond for him. When we first met this woman, she was spending a lot of money and was going out of her way to serve Elisha. She was full of life, confident, and seemed to be in control of everything. Now this woman was desperate and broken and Elisha wasn't throwing in the towel on her. The role had changed and now it was costing Elisha money and he was going out of his way to serve her. Why? [Because when you serve people with a generous spirit, they will want to serve you in the same manner.]

[Not all of the time, but usually, if you carry a servant's heart, believe in people, and find ways to take care of people, God sends people your way to take care of you.] Elisha went into that house that was full of hopelessness and started to pray. He started to pace and with each step of faith something came to life that seemed to be dead:

> He returned and walked back and forth in the house, and again went up and stretched himself out on him; then the child sneezed seven times, and the child opened his eyes. And he called Gehazi and said, "Call this Shunammite woman." So he called her. And when she came

in to him, he said, "Pick up your son." So she went in, fell at his feet, and bowed to the ground; then she picked up her son and went out.

(2 Kings 4:35–37 NKJV)

This Shunammite woman was about to plan a funeral service and instead, her dream was given new life. The Bible says she "went out." However, if you have kids, I'm sure she didn't just "go out" like you would leave Target. It's not like she just got what she needed and left. Her son was dead. Her dream of being a mother was gone. Her heart was shattered. Now she was leaving with her son and had a new hope for the future with him. You can only try to imagine the amount of tears the Shunammite woman cried when her son came back to life that soaked his shoulders. You can only try to picture what her face looked like as she left that place with her son.

I wish I could see what his father looked like when she returned home with her son. If it were my son, I would sprint across the driveway, tackle him, and ugly cry until he fought me off him. And even then, I wouldn't let him go.

This story has a happy ending. But not every story in life does. In fact, many heroes of faith died without seeing the full promise, which means their dreams didn't fully come true.

WHERE TO TURN WHEN WE FEEL LET DOWN

These all died in faith, not having received the promises, but having seen them afar off were assured of them, embraced them and confessed that they were strangers and pilgrims on the earth.

(Hebrews 11:13 NKJV)

Those who "died in faith" refer to all the heroes of faith. Yes, the ones who loved Jesus with all of their hearts and took gigantic steps of faith for Jesus died without receiving the full promise. The dream they had in their hearts never came full circle.

What do you do when God's promises seem unfulfilled? What is your response when something seems dead that you were believing for?

A dream. A marriage. A promise. A healing. A relationship.

What do you do?

Hope deferred makes the heart sick.

(Proverbs 13:12 NKJV)

Did you know it's okay to feel disappointment? You aren't any less spiritual because you feel let down. I hope that comforts you in some way. You don't lack faith when your heart hurts when a dream dies. It's a human expression. So many people's response is self-preservation. They say, "I'm just not going to get my hopes up anymore because every time I extend my faith I get let down. I'm not going to trust any more leaders because I've been let down. I'm not going to plant into a great church because it's not perfect. I'm not going to let anyone close because every time I let people in I get hurt."

So many people end up living with a pessimistic perspective in life. A friend wants to bless you and your first thought is, "Why bother? They must have an angle—they are trying to get something from me." A church is growing and you assume it must be one of those churches that doesn't preach the Bible. That person can't be that encouraging. They just want people to think they are perfect.

That family can't be that fun. They are hypocrites. Usually when that happens, one of the first things you stop doing is serving others because you are so afraid to get hurt again.

This woman was given this amazing gift of motherhood through serving. However, when life hurts, it can take all the joy out of serving others and we become self-consumed with our own problems. We stop serving in church because we can't get our eyes off of ourselves. We stop serving our families because we can't get our focus off of our pain. One of the first things to happen when life hurts most is we stop doing the things that give us the most joy.

These all died in faith, not having received the promises, but seeing them from afar off.

(Hebrews 11:13 NKJV)

A few things jump out at me when I read that verse. The first thing is it reminds me of the story we read about Jacob trying to get Rachel to Bethlehem. He was almost there but didn't quite make it. You can love God with all of your heart and not fully see the dream He's given you come true. The second thing that jumps out at me is that they didn't die with bitterness.

How did they die? In faith. That is huge! Those of us who have placed our hope in Jesus don't just die like the rest of the world. We live and die by faith.

If you are experiencing a partly fulfilled promise right now, you aren't alone. You are in good company. God hasn't abandoned you. You have a friend in Abraham, Moses, Isaac, Joseph, and many others throughout history. The only person who has ever lived that has died with total and complete fulfillment and finished work is Jesus Christ. When Jesus died He said, "It is finished."

So you're in good company. You aren't alone.

When you begin to understand that God is a generational God, it changes everything. It will change the way you serve and how you invest your life when you begin to understand that many times what God promised to Abraham, He fulfilled in Isaac. What He promised to Isaac, He fulfilled in Jacob. What He promised to Jacob, He fulfilled in Joseph. What He promises to Brian and Alicia, He will fulfill in my six kids, my grandkids, and all generations after us.

What you and I are walking through is never just about us. We serve a generational God and the part we play isn't as important as the story we are a part of. When Abraham died, God's people kept moving forward. When Joseph died, God's people kept moving forward. When Moses died, Joshua took God's people and kept moving forward. God's promises remain from season to season.

In the New Testament, the disciples died and the local churches continued to grow even more rapidly. When I retire someday, the church will go on. So we need to expand our view and understanding that the promises He's made to us will outlast us.

So the next time you feel that a dream is dead or that God hasn't fulfilled His promise, take those partially fulfilled promises back to the One who promised them. There are times in life, like that woman, where you need to keep pounding on heaven's door until you see your breakthrough. Don't give up just because it looks dead. And whatever happens, we have to trust that God is going to weave us into His place to reach more people who need this hope we have in Christ.

In the Old Testament, it seemed like almost every story had a happy ending. In the New Testament, it seemed like every story had a tragic ending. God doesn't always answer our prayers the way we hope He will. But when we can't understand His ways, we can always trust His heart.

Take every promise back to the Promiser. I love this story in 2 Kings. This woman is so authentic in her response. But instead of taking her promise back to the Promiser, to whom did she take it to? Elisha. Elisha was nothing special. He was just like you and me. It's God working through him that makes him such an influencer. Elisha couldn't do anything apart from God. She went to Elisha. Elisha understood the promise he gave wasn't his own, but from God. So Elisha took it to the Promiser.

This is so encouraging. Sometimes you need someone to stand in the gap for you when you don't have enough faith to pray yourself. Life is hard. Is it okay to just get that off our chest? Life is not fair; it's exhausting, and it's painful. All of us get to crossroads in our lives where we don't have the energy left to believe for our miracle. When those times come, it's so important that you have people around you willing to go to battle for you.

That doesn't make you any less spiritual. It makes you human.

Sarah thought it was about her son Isaac. Rebecca thought it was about her son Jacob. Leah thought it was about her son Reuben. Rachel thought it was about her son Joseph. Hannah thought it was about her son Samuel. And this Shunammite woman thought it was about her son. But it was never about the son. It was about *the* Son. Everything in the

Old Testament points us to the sum and substance of all promises, which is Jesus.

Parents, this is just a tiny glimpse at how easy it is to forget that our kids really aren't our kids. They belong to God and to be used for His glory and purpose in the earth.

Every dream, experience, and promise given to us is to move us toward Jesus.

I have come to believe that maybe this was never really about the boy coming back to life. Maybe this story was about Jesus and revealing His personhood to an entire community of people who were far from Him.

> For the Son of God, Jesus Christ, who was preached among you by us—by me and Silas and Timothy—was not "Yes" and "No," but in him it has always been "Yes." For no matter how many promises God has made, they are "Yes" in Christ. And so through him the "Amen" is spoken by us to the glory of God.

> (2 Corinthians 1:19–20)

Can you imagine how many people possibly came to know God in this woman's community when her son came back to life? I would like to think that there were a few people who were far from God who, through this woman's testimony, came to have a relationship with God because of this miracle.

Everything is for God's glory.

Let's read that last line of that verse.

"And so through him the 'Amen' is spoken by us to the glory of God."

This boy coming back to life was about God's glory. Jesus coming to Earth was for God's glory. The cross was all about God's glory. Our family that we have the privilege of serving is for God's glory. Our dreams that He gives us are for God's glory. The gifts we've been entrusted with are for God's glory. God who has healed my heart and freed me to forgive and believe the best in people is all for the glory of God.

Everything is for God's glory. We exist for Him. He does not exist for us.

We can be confident that we can take all our dreams and promises back to the Promiser.

Jack Hayford, pastor of The Church on the Way, once said: "Jesus is the fulfillment and fulfiller of all of God's promises because He is their sum and substance."

[Knowing that, you don't have to throw in the towel, close up, and become self-consumed. You can still serve in the middle of heartache and fight for the dream inside of your heart. In fact, there's something that happens in our hearts when we continue to serve in the middle of our brokenness that is powerful. God not only meets us in that place, but he uses us to reach others who are going through the same experiences we are.

You can still be happy when others experience breakthrough in the middle of waiting for your own. It's a heart posture that you choose to carry.]

I can't promise that you will get that house you always dreamed of, or you won't get passed up on that promotion you deserved. I can't promise that every time you pray for someone to be healed that they will be. I can't promise that nothing bad will ever happen to you because you love Jesus.

But I do know this . . . we are holding on to something so much more than just a promise. We are holding on to the Promiser.

[Every day we have the choice to pick up Jesus and choose to continue to serve even in the midst of pain and hardship. We have the choice to still be generous even when we feel like we don't have anything left to give.]

Parents, when life seems overwhelming, pick up Jesus and continue to speak life over your kids. Let them know they are known, prized, and marked by Majesty. Teach them to live for God's glory and not for the American dream. Teach them that when life doesn't go according to plan, they can take their dreams and promises back to the Promiser.

There's only one thing to do with a sick heart. There's only one place to turn when you have been left with disappointment. And that's to pick up the Son and cling to Jesus.

I don't have all the answers. I don't know why God spares some and lets others die. I don't know why He has allowed some to be born in America with a life full of opportunity and others in a country full of war. I don't know why some prayers are answered overnight and other prayers seem to go unanswered. I'm ok with saying I don't know. I'm not God. What I do know is He's faithful to fulfill His promise one way or another. God may not have always answered my prayers the way I felt they should have been answered. But it's always worked out for His glory.

Cling to Jesus!

Hold onto Him with everything you have. Don't stop serving God or others just because life hurts or you feel like a dream has died. Don't stop dreaming God-sized dreams just because you experienced some setbacks. Continue to trust in Jesus. When you look back at the end of your life, I promise you will be glad you placed all of your hope in Jesus.

I have never met anyone who was at the end of their life and regretted placing their hope in Jesus.

I'm certain that the heroes of faith aren't up in heaven saying, "I'm so disappointed. I wish I trusted less." So don't lose hope. Continue to believe for more. Trust Jesus to come through for you. Decide right now to let go of that offense and choose to forgive those who have wronged you. Step out and live a bold and courageous life. Dare to dream things for your life that are bigger than you.

At that the end of your life, when the curtain on your life closes, you will be able to look back and say, "Even if I don't see the full promise, what God started in me, He certainly will fulfill in the next generation."

I love what Brian Houston, pastor of Hillsong Church, once said: "I want my ceiling to be the next generation's floor to stand on."

To me, that's a life well lived!

7

love everyone, always

Let's face it. There will be days where life will break you down and you will have a freak-out moment. Anyone brave enough to admit that you have had a freak-out moment? It can be because finals are coming up, or you broke down in the middle of a snowstorm, or because your kids won't stop fighting, or because someone cut you off on the highway.

It doesn't matter what season of life you are in, we have all had a freak-out moment.

It's part of being human.

I'm not proud of my freak-out moments. I felt that one, however, was justified. I'm a pretty even-tempered person. But every man has his breaking point.

We had four kids at the time and were down at the Plaza in Kansas City on Black Friday, and it was a long day. Parents, you know what I'm talking about. From the moment we woke up we didn't stop shopping. Several hours later it was past dinner time, we hadn't eaten, the streets were crowded, the stores were packed, and we were still trying to find an outfit for the kids for our Christmas services. When I say "we," I really mean Alicia.

Alicia was in and out of the car going from store-to-store and everyone was ready to go home. By this point, I didn't care if we dressed them up in some onesies for Christmas.

Instead of embracing the moment and modeling patience for my children, I was starting to get irritable with Alicia and the kids. The kids were getting antsy in the car but Alicia wanted to go into the H&M clothing store one more time. We already had gone in that store earlier in the day, but Alicia wanted to go in one more time.

It is like going to the refrigerator several times hoping that the food has changed from the previous time you opened it. I was done. I wasn't going in one more store. I told her that I would stay in the car with the kids. My kids were little back then.

I thought by giving Alicia time to go into H&M that I would have time to catch a power nap. I assumed that by putting on a movie for my kids, they would have mercy on me and let their dad rest in peace. I couldn't have been more mistaken. Two minutes after Alicia left the car, my fourth born, Brooklyn, who was six months old at the time, started to scream. She didn't just do a normal scream. It was that type of scream that makes your brain hurt. She would not settle down.

I'm convinced she sensed fear in me. Her scream grew louder and louder. You would have thought I would have freaked out then. I didn't.

I was like, "Girl, go ahead and work out your lungs. I'm closing my eyes for a few minutes and you all are on your own."

Clearly that wasn't the smartest thing I've ever done as a parent. I shut my eyes and five minutes later I began to smell the worst smell I had ever smelled in my entire life. I have four kids. I'm not a stranger to odors. This one was different, though. I got so mad I didn't even address it. I didn't even turn around.

I just rolled down the window and said to myself, "There's no way I'm changing this one. I'm saving this one for Alicia."

Don't sit there and judge me.

Moms, don't pretend like you've never saved a dirty diaper for your husband when he walks in the door after a long day at work. That baby diaper is sagging to the floor, blown up like a balloon, and you are trying to pretend like it just happened.

I tried to wait out the smell but it kept getting worse—and then the kids start belly laughing. So now I have a screaming six-month-old and three other kids belly laughing. The smell got so bad that I had to address the problem.

What I didn't know was my son Riley, who was two years old at the time, had dug into his dirty diaper and acted like he was Picasso and finger painted with his "you know what" all over the car and his body.

When I say everywhere, I mean *everywhere*.

That was the final straw. I don't remember the last time I flipped out like that.

I went off.

"Are you kidding me, Riley? Come on. I don't care if you are two years old, you should know better," I started screaming.

Honestly, I wasn't even making sense. I just couldn't believe that Alicia was shopping while I was dealing with this mess.

By this point Alicia was on her way back to the parking garage and heard me having a melt down across the garage. What made it even worse was my kids weren't crying in fear. They were laughing at me. That just added fuel to the fire. Alicia came to the van and like any good wife she opened the car door, took one whiff of the smell and started dry heaving.

We looked like a circus.

Instead of relieving me, she took Brooklyn out of the car, closed the door, and left me all alone with the kids.

It was just me, Riley, and my two oldest daughters in the car. As I was changing Riley, he was staring at me with that look in his eye. I sensed he was up to something but I was so busy stripping him down and wiping off the windows that I wasn't even thinking straight. I started to calm down as I began to change him, but made a rookie mistake. I didn't wrap up the diaper when I took it off. I left it exposed. Riley sensed weakness so as hard as he could he kicked his heels up and down three time onto that soggy, wet diaper and splattered his "you know what" all over my clothes and lip.

That's right . . . some landed on my lip! I am embarrassed to admit that launched my second worst breakdown moment I've ever had. I lost it again. I couldn't catch a break. Of course, Alicia and the girls started laughing hysterically as Brooklyn was perfectly calm in momma's arms just staring at me. At that moment I was not grateful for the privilege of parenting. I was not in the mood for a hug, and the whole way home I was silent.

Alicia and I laugh about it now but I was so mad at the time that I cleaned up Riley with Alicia's scarf that she left in the car. It's not my proudest moment but it was my way of getting back at her for leaving a man behind.

Anyone ever been there?

It's easy to freak out when things change in our environment and we wish we were anywhere else but where we are at that moment. For me, this was an easy clean up. I changed his clothes, hosed him down at home, cleaned up the inside of my car, apologized to my wife and kids for responding poorly, and we moved on.

I want you to see that it may look like everything around us is crashing down and in chaos, but I promise you, God is in complete control. He isn't surprised or intimidated by anything that is happening in our world today.

God never has freak out moments!

I want to look at a Bible story that, if you grew up inside the walls of the church, you have probably heard a hundred times. If you're new in your walk with Jesus or haven't grown up in church, chances are you probably still have heard of this famous story.

> Among those who were chosen were some from Judah: Daniel, Hananiah, Mishael and Azariah. The chief official gave them new names: to Daniel, the name Belteshazzar; to Hananiah, Shadrach; to Mishael, Meshach; and to Azariah, Abednego. But Daniel resolved not to defile himself with the royal food and wine, and he asked the chief official for permission not to defile himself this way.

> (Daniel 1:6–8)

These young men were chosen. Let me set the background. There was a king in power at this time named King Nebuchadnezzar, an evil dictator and world conqueror. One day he came along this piece of land called Israel. So he began to put a plan together to invade Israel. While that was happening, a prophet from Israel named Jeremiah was speaking on God's behalf to a remnant of people who chose to embrace the life and purpose that God had for them. They were reflectors of God's goodness, faithfulness, and mercy.

Within that remnant there were four young men who belonged to four royal families: Daniel, Hananiah, Mishael, and Azariah. Historically naming someone during this time in history was very significant.

A lot has changed in our day and age. There's no shortage of creativity when it comes to naming our children.

Today parents name their kids after a family member or friend, or perhaps they Google the top names over the past year. Maybe that name has a cool meaning or maybe not. There's nothing wrong with that at all. However, in this time in history names were very significant. And it wasn't just a word. Often, they named them with a sentence.

Those families who were set apart for God would name their children for what they believed they were going to do for God. It was like a foresight into what they would become. That name would become their identity.

That is why when someone had a life-changing encounter with God in the Bible, many times God would change their name, signifying a new identity and mission had been given to them. We see this in both the Old and New Testament.

In those days, they would hold a public ceremony to name them. It's like a modern-day reveal party. It was a big deal. During this ceremony they named one boy Daniel, which means, "God is my judge." The second boy was named Hananiah. That name means, "The Lord shows grace." The third boy that is mentioned was named Mishael, which means, "Who is like God?" The last boy we learn of was named Azariah, which means, "The Lord helps."

These names were not speaking of their personalities. They were speaking more to who God was. It was as if these parents were speaking life over their children as to what they saw their sons becoming one day.

A CHOSEN GENERATION

As these four boys grew older, the prophet Jeremiah began mentoring these young men. The time finally came when Nebuchadnezzar invaded Israel, destroyed much of the land, and eventually captured Daniel, Hananiah, Mishael, and Azariah.

They were just fourteen years old.

Fourteen years old was the age the Babylonians entered men into their reeducation program to serve this evil king.

I can't imagine being just fourteen years old and having this happen to me.

These young teenagers were taken away from everything they've ever known to be conformed to the Babylonian people's belief system.

Serving God and others is in no way a get-out-of-jail-free card to suffering. The enemy of our souls is not going to roll out the red carpet for us to impact people and change our city.

Every time we begin to serve, live for Jesus, and gain ground for the kingdom of God, hell gets nervous and wants to take us out. So, by the king's order, his officials intentionally chose these young men among others.

Some of you may be thinking, "Wait a minute. Weren't these young men from families that were set apart for God? Weren't these young men pursuing God, in love with God, and standing for truth? Weren't these the teenagers making right choices and growing in their faith?

It's an honest emotion to ask these types of questions because we live in a culture where we say, "Jesus, I'll serve you but I have predetermined limits as to how far I'm willing to go."

As much as they loved God, they were chosen by this evil king; but the greater truth is they were already hand-picked and chosen by God before the king's officials ever laid eyes on them. They weren't taken from their families. God sent them. There's not one thing that can happen in the life of a believer that doesn't first pass through the hands of our Creator. He is not shocked or intimidated by anything going on in your life right now. There is no new information when it comes to God. There's a vast difference between walking outside of the grace of God and removing yourself from the protection of God because of habitual sin or an unrepentant heart, and what we are talking about here.

God was not freaking out. God was molding these young teenagers all those years to be sent to a people group because He knew there were teenagers, singles, and families far from Him that He needed to reach.

These four boys, along with others, were taken back to Babylon. Babylon was the center of all spiritualism at that time. It was a wicked and perverse environment. King Nebuchadnezzar was on the move to indoctrinate his culture and instill his beliefs into every land he conquered. He took these boys away from their culture, family, and everything they ever knew. He did this because he wanted to force them to take on his culture, gods, philosophies, and way of living. He was trying to strip them of everything they knew and believed.

What makes this story even more fascinating is that these four young men were from Judah. That's significant because Jesus would eventually come from Judah and there was a covenantal promise made to Abraham and David.

This is once again revealing to us that the enemy of our souls is hard at work trying to stop the plan and will of God in every generation. I hope you are starting to understand that this wasn't about Daniel, Hananiah, Mishael, and Azariah. Jesus was at the center of it all.

King Nebuchadnezzar destroyed much of the geographical area of Judah and also destroyed the temple of God. Now his plan was to destroy the people of Judah's identity.

So these four young teenagers, along with many others, would train for three years in Babylonian language and literature and enter into the king's service for the purpose of sending them back into their city as Babylonian leaders.

Even the enemy understands the power of servanthood.

I can't prove this, but I would assume this had to be the worst season in these young men's lives up to this point. Stop and really think about what just happened to them; they were due for a freak-out moment.

Daniel, Hananiah, Mishael, and Azariah were taken from their family and friends. They were removed from Jeremiah, their spiritual leader and pastor. They no longer had their church to encourage them. They no longer had their family to turn to. They didn't have the worship band inspiring their heart.

These young men were on their own, and their faith would be tested.

Through all of these challenges, in the face of this difficult moment, they gave up their right to freak out and continued to trust God in the middle of this wicked nation.

I don't know about you, but I'm challenged looking at such great faith!

It made King Nebuchadnezzar angry. His plan wasn't working.

So King Nebuchadnezzar came up with a genius plan. He realized that to make the greatest impact on their lives, he had to try to strip them of their identity. So he decided to separate them and change their names. Together they could still encourage one another, but if he separated them, he had a better chance at changing their hearts.

Nebuchadnezzar took Daniel and linked him to one of the gods of Babylon named Bel and changed his name from Daniel to Belteshazzar, which means, "Bel protect his life." Then he took Hananiah to the temple of Aku which was a moon god and changed his name from Hananiah, which means, "The Lord is gracious," to Shadrach, which means, "Command of Aku." Then he took Mishael to a temple full of perversion and renamed him Meshack meaning, "Who is what Aku is?" Finally he took the last boy, Azariah, and renamed him Abednego, which means, "Servant of Nego."

Notice that the enemy isn't very creative. He was just trying to copy and pervert what God had already spoken over their life. Each of these young men was tied to the gods that the Babylonians worshiped.

You and I are reading this story and thinking, "How in the world did these young men not have a freak-out moment?"

I would be like, "God. Hello? Are you seeing this? May I offer some constructive suggestions in your planning process? I know it's a new generation and things like this may have worked out in Noah's day. But your methods seem a bit outdated. Let me catch you up on how this works."

However, notice that these men had such a sense of honor that even when this evil king took everything they had they did not act like victims of what had been done to them or prisoners to their environment. They did not take shots at the leadership in office. They weren't disgusted with the culture they were thrown into.

Just let that sink in for a second.

They didn't hate the Babylonian people. The Babylonian people didn't know God. They were born into that lifestyle. It's all they knew. What if these young men could make a difference in this culture by being faithful and serving without compromising who they were? I'm convinced that when you know who Jesus is, you see who He's calling you to be wherever you find yourself.

This doesn't happen by living on rumors of who Jesus is. If you follow Jesus based on rumors of who He is, when life gets tough, you are going to have a lot of freak-out moments. When you actually know Him and get to be familiar with His character and calling on your life, you realize He is actually sending you to people who do not know Him.

Understanding who Jesus really is determines how we live and how we see ourselves.

It changes our perception of how we live our lives.
It changes how we view our finances.
It changes how we serve those around us.

Truth be told, these young men weren't really taken from their homes. They were sent! God had a plan for these four boys because the plan was all about God reaching people who were far from Him. God knew people would be watching. The king failed to realize that God wasn't bound to a geographical location, or held captive by the temple walls. Nebuchadnezzar didn't realize God shined and moved through history through His people.

God was actually planting His followers in that city:

- Men He could trust to carry His Name and honor Him in the middle of a perverse generation
- Men who worked hard and had a great attitude, and were attractional leaders who didn't freak out in moments of difficulty and uncertainty
- Leaders who weren't distracted by the cravings of this world
- Leaders He knew would not be so easily offended by their environment and take everything personally because they knew God was actually the one in control of the outcome
- Leaders whose identity was in the God of Israel

These young men had no expiration date when it came to how far they were willing to go to serve God.

I think many of us, if we are honest with ourselves, have un-voiced and pre-determined limits as to how far we are willing to go or what we're willing to do in the King's service. Many people won't say it because they wouldn't sound as spiritual, but they've intentionally or unintentionally placed an expiration time table of how far they are willing to serve, give, or love people based on a number of criteria:

We are willing to love anyone . . . who share our beliefs.
We are willing to serve anyone . . . that votes like us.
We are willing to go anywhere . . . that has a great school system.
We are willing to take a risk on people . . . that have our same color skin.

God is looking for servant-leaders in every generation who will use their gifts, money, time, and resources for His glory to reach people far from Him.

God is looking for people who will see through eyes of grace and compassion. People who will love the unlovable.

These young men were saying, "You can try and change our names, but you will never be able to change who we really are."

God deeply loved the people in this city—not their actions, but them!

For God so loved the world, that whosoever believes in me will not perish but have everlasting life.

(John 3:16)

He so loved the world. Wow! Who did He love? The "whosoevers."

Even Jesus, the Son of God, was sent to save you and me.

You see, before we met Jesus, you and I were just like the people of Babylon. We were lost and dead in our sin. And someone had to come to us and save us.

That person was Jesus. He left the comfort of heaven, where there was no shortage of worship, to come down to rescue you and me.

You and me don't get to determine who the whosoevers are.

For generations we have had religious people trying to set up a check-list as to whom God can save and whom God can't save.

VIVE Culture will fight for every person's right to have a place at the foot of the cross because we know Jesus fought for us to have a place there. There are no categories. Jesus took the VIP rope down and has allowed us to find grace, truth, and love through Jesus.

Thank God that Jesus sent His Son to save us.

But God demonstrates His own love toward us, in that while we were still sinners, Christ died for us.

(Romans 5:8 NKJV)

That means when you were living a perverse life and serving the gods on this age, Jesus was sent to rescue you. Jesus served the mission of His Father so you and I could be saved. Praise God!

You can't really reach people you don't love. It's when you realize that you, too, were once were in that place—if not for grace—that a passion in you will ignite to run to your city with the hope of Jesus.

God loves the whosoevers and is willing to take us out of our comfort zones and risk our nice clean reputations as Christians, for His Name's sake. It's much more than attending a church service, singing songs, and filling your head up with head knowledge.

The proof is in the living.

The proof is in the sending.

The health of any church isn't reflected in the seating capacity. It's in sending capacity. The proof of a true disciple of Jesus isn't how many church services you attend, or how many Bible verses you can memorize, or how many books you have read. Simply talking about Jesus isn't the goal. I know a lot of people who want to impress people with their head knowledge but aren't reaching anyone for Jesus. They are more inter-ested in showing off how smart they are than actually loving people.

We all know the people I'm referring to. They sit around trying to be modern-day theologians, but at the same time, most people can't stand to be around them.

The fruit of the righteous is a tree of life, and he who wins souls is wise.

(Proverbs 11:30 NKJV)

I'm so thankful that Jesus came to seek and save that which was lost. There's not one person on this planet that doesn't fall into that category. All of us were lost, broken, and disconnected from the heart of God if not for His grace coming to us. Grace isn't us coming to God. It's God coming to us through His Son Jesus. And we are called to this harvest field in this generation to be God's agents of grace. You will never worship God with a sincere heart, or love people unconditionally as the Father does, or be willing to go wherever to whomever until you properly understand how much you are indebted to His mercy and grace. That revelation changes everything.

Jesus didn't come to make bad people good. He came to make dead people live.

Jesus came to save us from every single sinful thought, word, or deed we've done.

Let's be honest with ourselves. No one has ever really heard our real testimony.

They know the PG version that is church-appropriate. Jesus has seen it all and still came running toward you.

These four young men may have been called by their Babylonian name but they knew who they really were.

They were like, "You can call me Beltashazar, but I'm Daniel."

"You can call me Shadrach but my name is Hananiah."

As you continue to follow their journey, you would think that they would just cave in and burn out. What we learn, though, is God began to give them influence by serving the king.

That is just incredible to me.

WILL THE REAL FOLLOWERS OF JESUS
PLEASE STAND UP?

Like anyone in power, King Nebuchadnezzar needed an ego boost. So he sent out a decree that everyone must worship his gods and his idol that was built. Anyone who failed to do so would be thrown in a burning fire. Again, I'm not sure how these young men didn't freak out.

One time I burned my finger on my wife's flat iron that she had warming up on the bathroom sink and I thought my hand was going to have to be amputated. I soaked it for hours as I asked Siri with my other hand how to cure first-degree burns.

These young men inspire me. God sets the stage because He knew He would have this nation's undivided attention.

These young men knew they were sent to impact this culture. However, there came a time where they would have to put their popularity and reputations on the line to stand for truth.

In our day in age, that means a time comes in all of our lives where Christian leaders will have to put their book sales on the line to speak truth. Pastors will have to risk their social media followers to stand for truth.

There always comes a time where there is a clear line drawn between what we stand for as opposed to what the world does. In no way does this mean we are against the person. You can stand against what someone believes but not be against the person.

You and I can differ on things but I still love you as a person.

However, there comes a point when my love for God has to trump my love for how you feel about me. My loyalty to God's Word and His way of living has to eclipse my desire for people's approval.

Shadrach, Meshach, and Abednego loved God so much that they could not worship Nebuchadnezzar's gods and idols. This means there will come a time where you, too, will have to make the decision to actually stand for truth, even if it isn't culturally popular or politically correct.

Nebuchadnezzar said to them, "Is it true, Shadrach, Meshach and Abednego, that you do not serve my gods or worship the image of gold I have set up? Now when you hear the sound of the horn, flute, zither, lyre, harp, pipe and all kinds of music, if you are ready to fall down and worship the image I made, very good. But if you do not worship it, you will be thrown immediately into a blazing furnace. Then what god will be able to rescue you from my hand?"

Shadrach, Meshach and Abednego replied to him, "King Nebuchadnezzar, we do not need to defend ourselves before you in this matter. If we are thrown into the blazing furnace, the God we serve is able to deliver us from it, and he will deliver us from Your Majesty's hand. But even if he does not, we want you to know, Your Majesty, that we will not serve your gods or worship the image of gold you have set up."

(Daniel 3:14–18)

Nebuchadnezzar knew the answer to every question he was asking. He knew they didn't worship his gods or idols. That isn't what jumps out to me. What jumps out to me is they didn't feel the need to have to defend themselves.

In other words, they weren't easily offended. They were not getting all riled up trying to make a point to show everyone up. There are so many people who are easily offended at everything people do in our culture. Why? Chill out. These young men already knew that if it came down to it, they were willing to give their lives for what they believed. With every opportunity they would be faithful to serve, as long as it didn't require them to compromise their beliefs.

Once that ultimatum was given, they could not bow to comfort and convenience.

Cause over comfort.

They didn't have to pray about it or have a staff meeting about it.

Can I have an honest moment with you for a second?

Sometimes I look around and I can't tell the difference between pastors who lead churches, and people in the world.

We live in such a celebrity-driven culture that I believe there is a danger to trying to be so loved and accepted by everybody that we really don't stand for anything.

There are times when I hear influential leaders say things that grieve my heart. I understand everyone is on a journey and we need to have more conversations with people as opposed to simply making blanket statements.

I believe we are far too quick to judge others, and don't take enough time to really love people through the process. The painful struggles of life can't always be fixed with a black and white statement. We need to love people through their questions, frustrations, and life experiences.

In saying that, when it comes to clear standards that God has set in place, the most loving thing we can do to serve people is stand on God's Word and not sugarcoat how devastating sin really is.

Take abortion for example. Please stay with me on this point and hear my heart because I don't want to lose you.

I have walked teens through the painful regret of choosing to have an abortion. I have walked family members through the unbearable heartache of having their family members choose to have an abortion. During those moments, we have hurt with them, we've cried with them, and we've done our best to help guide them through the healing process.

It's one of the painful decisions that seem to impact a family for decades. Just because we have disagreed with the act of abortion doesn't mean we didn't care for the person. We loved them through the entire process and help connect them to professionals who could help them deal with the aftermath that stays with a person who chooses to have one.

That decision never really leaves a person, ever.

But if someone ever asks where VIVE stands when it comes to abortion, it isn't even up for discussion. We must stand with the Bible, even though it isn't politically correct.

It's not just wrong, it's murder.

This generation talks about social justice more than any other generation in history. Well, abortion is part of social justice. You want to be passionate about something? What defines social justice more than defending a human life that can't defend itself? What is more just than fighting for a human being who can't speak up or stand up for itself?

That's just one example.

I know that opens us up for ridicule and we could lose a lot of our social media followers and possible friendships, but there's a time to sit down and have a conversation, and then there's a time to stand for truth.

At VIVE Culture, we want our community to be in the world. Not *of* the world, but *in* the world and impacting and influencing culture. We believe we are called to our zip codes and communities and we consider it an honor to share life with so many people who look and think differently around us.

But at the end of the day, we have to have such a deep allegiance to the authority of God's Word and such a deep understanding of who we are in Christ that we can never bow to the gods of this world no matter how unpopular that makes us.

These three young men had to make a decision. Would they stand for truth? Or would they convince themselves they could influence society better by blending in?

The three young men put it all on the line.

They chose to stand up.

In our day in age, they would have been ripped to pieces on social media. They would have been trending on Twitter as bigots.

Mostly likely, they would have had their publishers cut ties with them and their endorsers run for the hills. They made an unpopular decision to choose Jesus over everything.

What an amazing way to live our lives.

The line that pierced my soul the most from those verses was when they said, "Even if God doesn't come through for us . . ."

That's faith. That's serving a greater mission. That's bigger than just attending a church service or being part of the worship team.

God, even if you don't heal my grandma, even if you don't heal that relationship, even if you don't allow the house to close, even if you don't . . . we will never turn our hearts from you.

If God hadn't sent them, an entire nation wouldn't have been able to witness this. However, a nation heard the gospel because a few men remained faithful and didn't have a freak-out moment. It's not recorded, but knowing the grace of Jesus, I've got to believe people at that moment were introduced to Jesus. People are looking for authenticity in this world. When you see that kind of faith, it changes people's lives.

We are a walking billboard of God's grace in our lives.

The enemy is still up to the same old tricks. He is out to destroy families and rob you and me of our God-given purpose. He is stripping millions of people of who they really were meant to be. When you are living with purpose, and really serving your generation, criticism is no longer personal. It's not about you. It's about Jesus.

"I served the Lord with great humility and with tears and in the midst of severe testing by the plots of my Jewish opponents. I only know that in every city the Holy Spirit warns me that prison and hardships are facing me. But none of these things move me; nor do I count my life dear to myself, so that I may finish my race with joy, and the ministry which I received from the Lord Jesus, to testify to the gospel of the grace of God."

(Acts 20:19, 23–24)

When God called me out of a life of sin and called me into ministry in the local church, I was like, "Are you out of options? Certainly there are others more qualified." I wish I could say that I've always stood up when I needed to stand for truth. If I did, I would be lying. There have been times where I've caved in to the pressure of the moment and walked away knowing I missed my chance to stand for truth.

There have been times where I knew I should have spoken up but instead remained silent because I was afraid of the backlash I would have to deal with. There have been times where I've taken a stand and times where I've missed my chance, but this is what I've learned over the years: I would rather be in the fire with Jesus than out of the fire without Him.

And if I'm going to have to be in the fire, I will choose to worship in the fire. Because when we stand for Jesus, we know that we are never alone. He is right there with us ready to make His Name great to those we are sent to serve.

Then Nebuchadnezzar was furious with Shadrach, Meshach and Abednego, and his attitude toward them changed. He ordered the furnace heated seven times hotter than usual and commanded some of the strongest soldiers in his army to tie up Shadrach, Meshach and Abednego and throw them into the blazing furnace. So these men, wearing their robes, trousers, turbans and other clothes, were bound and thrown into the blazing furnace. The king's command was so urgent and the furnace so hot that the flames of the fire killed the soldiers who took up Shadrach, Meshach and Abednego, and these three men, firmly tied, fell into the blazing furnace.

Then King Nebuchadnezzar leaped to his feet in amazement and asked his advisers, "Weren't there three men that we tied up and threw into the fire?" They replied, "Certainly, Your Majesty." He said, "Look! I see four men walking around in the fire, unbound and unharmed, and the fourth looks like a son of the gods."

Nebuchadnezzar then approached the opening of the blazing furnace and shouted, "Shadrach, Meshach and Abednego, servants of the Most High God, come out! Come here!" So Shadrach, Meshach and Abednego came out of the fire, and the satraps, prefects, governors and royal advisers crowded around them. They saw that the fire had not harmed their bodies, nor was a hair of their heads singed; their robes were not scorched, and there was no smell of fire on them.

Then Nebuchadnezzar said, "Praise be to the God of Shadrach, Meshach and Abednego, who has sent his angel and rescued his servants! They trusted in him and defied the king's command and were willing to give up their lives rather than serve or worship any god except their own God.

(Daniel 3:19–28)

This is a powerful story with so many lessons! King Nebuchadnezzar went ballistic. He had his strongest soldiers tie the men up so tight there was no possible way they could escape the flames. He had the fire turned up so hot that the flames killed the soldiers who threw Shadrach, Meshach, and Abednego into the furnace.

If the flames killed the soldiers and they were out of the furnace, shouldn't Shadrach, Meshach, and Abednego have been killed, too, before they were thrown in?

The answer is obviously yes.

But when the king looked inside this furnace, he no longer saw three men in there. He saw four. And Shadrach, Meshach, and Abednego weren't tucked away in the corner sucking their thumb complaining about God abandoning them.

Rather, they realized God was right next to them—so much so that the only thing burned was the rope constraining them. Just the fact that they didn't have any smell of fire on them reveals to us that there was a hedge of protection around them that this evil king couldn't touch.

"No weapon formed against you shall prosper, and every tongue which rises against you in judgment You shall condemn. This is the heritage of the servants of the Lord, and their righteousness is from Me," says the Lord.

(Isaiah 54:17 NKJV)

That is our heritage as the children of God. When He calls us to serve our family, coworkers, and cities, He will put a hedge of protection around us that the enemy can't touch. Our kids, coworkers, neighbors, and family members are watching how we respond to the challenges of this world.

I have to believe that when those three men came out of the fire, they were glowing–not glowing with pride ready to say, "I told you! Jesus get them!" They were glowing from being in the presence of Jesus. Who knows? Maybe when they heard the king call them out they didn't want to come out of that fire!

Would you? They were in the presence of God! I can tell you one thing is certain: there is no substitute for the presence of Jesus. There are not enough vacations on Earth that can replenish your soul like His presence. There are not enough college scholarships big enough to forfeit your kids' spiritual walk for. There are not enough Sundays to sleep in that would be worth not being planted in a local church every weekend.

When you begin to practice the presence of Jesus, you begin to crave His presence. That's one of the reasons I love the local church so much. Every single Sunday we can come together and get a taste of what heaven is going to be like. When you get time in Jesus' presence, things change.

Your heart posture changes.

How you speak about others changes.

The way you walk through challenges changes.

The way you parent and love your spouse changes.

These three men walked out of that fire, and knowing how God works, I would bet anything that families were saved that day. No, there weren't alter calls recorded but I know one thing . . . a nation was watching what had just occurred. You can't watch the miracle of three men walking out of a burning furnace unharmed and not be changed.

Families were forever changed that day that would have never been introduced to the God of Israel if those men weren't sent to this city. The story of these brave young men was never the central theme.

It was always about Jesus.

Our lives as followers of Jesus always have been, and will be about Jesus.

If you stay close to Jesus, you can serve everyone around you and not be burned out by people. You can serve this generation, as wicked as it can be at times, and remain full of faith.

I pray at the end my life my kids can watch my wife and me finish our race, not burned out and bitter, but still full of vision, hope, and joy. I want them to see that it is a privilege to serve our world. I want them to see through eyes of generosity and grace. I want them to live with a spirit of honor. If God allows it, I want to be an eighty-five-year-old man, with Alicia by my side, and my kids and grandbabies all around me, still full of vision for the city I live in.

IT'S NOT US vs. THEM

When we walk the streets of our city, what are we going to see? Them? Or do we see us? God doesn't see them. He sees His sons and daughters who are sick, hurting, and lost. Phil Yancey, an American Christian author, said it so well when he said: "The message of the Bible in one sentence—God wants His family back." God put you in that family. God put you in your city. God gave you that child. At VIVE Culture, these are our friends, family members, and coworkers. This is our city.

People are watching how we live, what we prioritize, how honest we are at work, how we talk about others, how we treat our family members and those closest to us, how we honor others, and so on. Too often we equate being moved with actually doing something. Hearts that are touched must move our hands and feet to action. I am living proof of His grace.

I love the story we just read because these young men never made it about us versus them. That means you can love and serve people who have a completely different way of living than you do. It's not about trying to fix anyone. No one is a project. You can't really impact people you don't truly love. When you really love people and love the generation you are part of, you can serve with no strings attached.

If you've given your heart to Christ, you have been given a new identity. Consider what the apostle Paul wrote:

Praise be to the God and Father of our Lord Jesus Christ, who has blessed us in the heavenly realms with every spiritual blessing in Christ.

(Ephesians 1:3)

What a good and generous Father to give every child of God every spiritual blessing through Christ. But the blessings are just a bonus. The real prize is Jesus. If Jesus didn't answer one more of our prayers in our lifetime, what He did on the cross over two thousand years ago would be more than enough to give Him our entire heart. Not only did He take our place and absorb all our sin, shame, and rebellion, He also gave us access to the throne room of heaven and every spiritual blessing is now ours through Jesus.

There is not a word in the entire world that can accurately describe how amazing, wonderful, and generous the love of God really is.

So no matter what is going on around you, or what's been done to you, you can stand confidently that God is able to come through one way or another because of who you are in Christ. The enemy may be trying to strip away who God has called you to be, but you can stand confidently in our God who is for you, with you, and leading you. He is positioning you, in whatever you are facing, to reach someone right here in this city that is watching and needs hope.

You may not be going through anything right now, but someone around you may need to borrow your faith for a little while until they are strong enough on their own. I want to remind you that God is madly in love with you. He's come to help you. You can be that father or mother He's called you to be. You can be an influencer in society without conforming to it.

You can serve and honor our leaders, no matter what side of the political spectrum they belong to, without selling out to the policies they may stand for. You can love that difficult person in your life without carrying an offense. You can choose to forgive that person who took advantage of you because you know what God did for you is greater than anything anyone has ever done to you.

You can live this way when you stay close to Jesus. Stay planted in the House. May we never lose our wonder of who He is and what He means to us.

Stay connected to other men and women who share the same passions and values as you do.

Stay humble and hungry for the things of God.

When you do, you won't see us versus them. You will see that we are sent to serve our generation so that people far from Jesus can experience the same love, forgiveness, and grace that we've experienced.

I don't know about you, but I don't just want to read about revival . . . I want to live it! My prayer is for us to see a move of God like never before. And Jesus, may it start in us first.

8

nothing is ever wasted

I love Oprah. There's something about her smile and spirit that I just love. I have never met her but when she talks, she is captivating to listen to. There was a commercial that went viral of her talking about her weight loss journey. There was a moment when she looked at the camera and with passion in her eyes said, "I love bread!"

I actually shouted, "Amen!" when I heard it for the first time. I'm Italian. I don't just like bread. I love bread. It's such a gift from heaven. Our family can't get enough of it.

I'm not sure how your house is but in Italian homes, we have bread with almost every meal during the week. In fact, we'll be waiting for dinner and we'll have bread on the counter to snack on. We love to dip it in oils, sauces, and Ranch dressing. We don't care; we just love to eat it. At times my kids love to grab a handful of Italian bread when they run by just to snack on throughout the day.

If you don't love bread you won't understand this—but for those of us who walk just a little bit closer to Jesus, you know even the smell of fresh baked bread kicks something inside of your soul and you can sense God is at work. The smell of fresh-baked bread is good for the soul. I'll take it a step further. I have certain places that we get our bread from. Not every store makes the same quality of bread. I'll admit it—I'm a bread snob.

I know the hot spots. When I get Italian bread at the store, I have to squeeze the bread and do a stale taste.

Anyone know what a stale test is?

A stale test is when you see steam on the paper and you gently squeeze the bread two or three times in different spots. If it's soft through the entire loaf, you know it's fresh. If it's hard in any spots, you know that was yesterday's leftovers. If it has a 50 percent off sticker on it, you know that's last week's bread. If you don't learn anything else in this chapter, you will walk away with your life forever changed just by that little bit of information.

Yes, Oprah, we agree. We love bread, too. When I think about serving with what we've been entrusted with, I can't help but think of a young boy in Mark Chapter 6. This young boy wasn't a giant, skilled warrior, theologian, or great king like we've seen in the past chapters. Young person, don't ever think you are too young to be a difference maker with what you've been given.

The apostles [who had been sent out on a mission] gathered together with Jesus and told Him everything that they had done and taught. He said to them, "Come away by yourselves to a secluded place and rest a little while"—for there were many [people who were continually] coming and going, and they could not even find time to eat.

And they went away by themselves in the boat to a secluded place. Many [people] saw them leaving, and recognized them and ran there together on foot from all the [surrounding] cities, and got there ahead of them. When Jesus went ashore, He saw a large crowd [waiting], and He was moved with compassion for them because they were like sheep without a shepherd [lacking guidance]; and He began to teach them many things. When the day was nearly gone, His disciples came to Him and said, "This is an isolated place, and it is already late; send the crowds away so that they may go into the surrounding countryside and villages and buy themselves something to eat."

(Mark 6:30–36 AMP)

Basically, Jesus' disciples were trying to tell Him that peoples' needs were someone else's problem. Notice that the disciples were sent out on mission. They were sent and excited about it. They felt great about coming back and bragging about the miracles that they had experienced. Now, it was after hours. Ministry hours were closed. I love how Jesus responded to them:

> But He replied, "You give them something to eat!" And they asked Him, "Shall we go and buy 200 denarii worth of bread and give it to them to eat?"

> (Mark 6:37 AMP)

200 denarii would be like a half a year's wages for us today. That is a huge sacrifice. Now, Jesus began to ask them to serve and give at a level that would cost them something:

> He said to them, "How many loaves do you have? Go look!" And when they found out, they said, "Five [loaves], and two fish."

> (Mark 6:38 AMP)

In John 6:9 we learn that the disciples were given a small boy's lunch to use. Mark continued, writing:

> Then Jesus commanded them all to sit down by groups on the green grass. They sat down in groups of hundreds and of fifties [so that the crowd resembled an orderly arrangement of colorful garden plots]. Taking the five loaves and two fish, He looked up to heaven and said a blessing [of praise and thanksgiving to the Father]. Then He broke the loaves and [repeatedly] gave them to the disciples to set before the people; and He divided up the two fish among them all. They all ate and were satisfied. And the disciples picked up twelve full baskets of the broken pieces [of the loaves], and of the fish. Those who

ate the loaves were five thousand men [not counting the women and children].

(Mark 6:39-44 AMP)

EVERYONE HAS SOMETHING GOD CAN USE

The disciples came back and were telling of all that they were doing and giving an account and they were excited. Word got out where Jesus was and they said five thousand men gathered. Back then, they would only count the men—but if you included the women and children, historians tell us there was a minimum of fifteen thousand in numbers. Think about that for a second. Before there were any mass mailers, social media promotions, or billboards, the word got out to what Jesus was doing and people began to discover how great, loving, and generous He was. This happened because the people of God began serving.

The disciples didn't need a budget or their own building to serve.

When lives start to be turned on to the gospel and hearts are truly changed, people start showing up and begin to tell everyone they know what Jesus has done.

What do you do when fifteen thousand people show up?

Me?

I start thinking about all the logistics. Do we have enough pens? Are the bathrooms clean? Do we have enough workers for the Kid's check-in station?

Jesus' mindset was different. He had compassion on them. Any miracle that has ever happened or will happen starts with compassion. Any healthy church that is planted or a new campus that is launched starts with compassion for a city or community.

The whole Bible is a story of God's compassion on us. So Jesus began to preach to them, and like some preachers, He was apparently long-winded because the crowds started to get hungry.

So one of his team members said, and I'm paraphrasing of course: "If you want people to come back next weekend, send them away to eat. Save point sixty-three for another day."

Jesus, being the compassionate leader that He was, looked at them and said, "You give them food."

In other words, Jesus was saying, "You serve them. We have every-thing we need right here to serve these people."

Let's be real. Most of us would respond like, "What do you mean me go serve them? Food distribution isn't in my job description. Those people aren't part of my zip code. They aren't my types of people."

The disciples didn't realize that if they were too big to serve, they were too small to lead. You never graduate from serving. We say the same things today, don't we?

I don't have those kinds of resources to give.
I don't have that kind of talent to offer.
I don't have enough time.
I don't have enough influence.

I don't care how much a person loves God there comes a time where most everyone tries to remind God that they are not enough.

I remember the moment I clearly heard God speak to my heart that it was time to move on from the church we were serving in and it was time to run with the vision to lead our own church like He first spoke to our hearts when we first got married. When we began to get an idea of what the mission looked like in Kansas City, and how much need there really was in our city, we felt completely overwhelmed.

I can't speak for my wife, but I know I was so full of fear. We didn't have a name for our church, a church bank account, an EIN number, or anyone on our team. And before we told a soul we had to get to a place where we were willing to go even if we went alone. Even if no one got behind us, we were all in. The needs were just too great to stay put because it was comfortable and convenient.

We understand that God doesn't need us. His plans aren't hinged on if Brian and Alicia Rose say yes. He will fulfill His purpose for our city one way or another. He didn't need us. We needed Him. We wanted in. Whatever God was up too, our hands were raised to be sent. We didn't know everything, but we knew one thing: God could start with eight people to serve Kansas City—me, my wife, and six kids.

That's all we had.

It wasn't easy—especially when people were trying to talk us out of something God clearly had called us to. In those moments, you have to stay so close to Jesus that you can't let someone else's vision for your life trump what God's vision is.

We didn't have a vision. We believe God's vision had us.

There comes a time where you have to stop with the excuses as to why you can't step out and serve the needs around you. The spirit of a difference maker starts with simple acts of obedience—not someone who sees the end results first, but someone willing to take one step at a time. It begins with extravagant faith.

Some of the most exciting times in life happen when we are forced out into the wild blue yonder.

The ingredients for our miracles to serve our generation are always in our midst. The seed never looks like the harvest it contains.

I have learned that you always reap what you sow. But you don't always reap a harvest in the *place* you sow. So many times because we can't do everything a lot of people end up doing nothing. What do you have? Do you think only one little boy had a lunch? No. But can you imagine the one boy in a crowd of fifteen thousand people who said, "You can have my lunch."

Picture that moment.

There is something powerful about a young person who says yes to Jesus at an early age.

Jesus can do something when you step into the yes. All we've got to serve God with on this side of eternity is our time, treasure, and talent. We spend so much of our time devaluing what we don't have. We say things like, "If I just had their church, home, marriage, upbringing, budget or resources, or worship experience, then I could . . ."

God never asks us for what someone else has. He asked, "What do *you* have?"

Don't minimize small beginnings.

Impossible is where God starts. Jesus took what was not enough and He blessed it. That little boy's lunch was never supposed to be enough. What if, instead of devaluing our "not enough," we changed our confession and spoke life over what we've been given?

To me, the power of this story isn't even in what they ate. The power of the story is what was left in scraps.

NOTHING IS EVER WASTED

And they all ate and were satisfied.

(Mark 6:42 AMP)

That is incredible that approximately fifteen thousand people were satisfied. So much so, that there were even leftovers. Jesus could have told the disciples to leave the leftovers. But nothing is ever wasted in the hands of Jesus. The Bible says that Jesus had them pick up twelve baskets full of leftovers before they got back into the boat:

And the disciples picked up twelve full baskets of the broken pieces [of the loaves], and of the fish. Those who ate the loaves were five thousand men [not counting the women and children].

(Mark 6:43-44 AMP)

How many baskets? Twelve.
How many disciples? Twelve.
Every one of the disciples took a basket with them in the boat.

The number twelve is so significant in the Bible. The number twelve is a symbol of faith. The book of Genesis states there were twelve sons of Jacob and those twelve sons formed the twelve tribes of Israel. In the New Testament, Jesus was twelve years old when He questioned the scholars in the temple. When it was time for Jesus' ministry to begin, He chose twelve disciples to pour His life into. According to the book of Revelation, the kingdom of God has twelve gates guarded by twelve angels. The number twelve appears one hundred and eighty-seven times in the Bible.

Jesus could have said, "Leave the scraps. I'll whip up a magic trick at a later date." But He needed them to pick up the evidence of the miracle He did that day so they could carry it into the storm of tomorrow. Because when life gets hard, and it will, you can look down to those scraps and declare that the same God who was with you on the mountain top is the same God that will be with you in the storm.

The disciples were front and center experiencing this historic miracle, but they missed the whole point of the miracle altogether. We serve and see God move in powerful ways in other people's lives, but how often do we doubt His presence when we are walking through our own storms?

The disciples were in awe of the miracle, but Jesus wanted them in awe of the Miracle Maker. If you are in awe of a miracle, that will last for a moment. When you are in awe of the Miracle Maker it changes your life.

Jesus immediately insisted that His disciples get into the boat and go ahead [of Him] to the other side to Bethsaida, while He was dismissing the crowd. And after He said goodbye to them, He went to the mountain to pray. Now when evening had come, the boat was in the middle of the sea, and Jesus was alone on the land. Seeing the disciples straining at the oars, because the wind was against them, at about the fourth watch of the night (3:00-6:00 a.m.) He came to them, walking on the sea. And [acted as if] He intended to pass by them. But when they saw Him walking on the sea, they thought it was a ghost, and cried out [in horror]; for they all saw Him and were shaken and terrified.

But He immediately spoke with them and said, "Take courage! It is I (I Am)! Stop being afraid." Then He got into the boat with them, and the wind ceased [as if exhausted by its own activity]; and they were completely overwhelmed, because they had not understood [the miracle of] the loaves [how it revealed the power and deity of Jesus]; but [in fact] their heart was hardened [being oblivious and indifferent to His amazing works].

(Mark 6:45–52 AMP)

Unbelievable.

I don't say that in a way that looks down at the disciples. I say that because I see myself in that story so many times. I can't tell you how many times I've had spiritual amnesia where God does an amazing work in and through my life, and in the middle of a storm I panic and start trying to work in my own strength instead of looking to Jesus.

Jesus is so amazing that He knows that our human nature will always pull us toward what we only see as possible. That is why Jesus tells us to pick up our scraps from the miracles of the past. Those same scraps that are with us on the mountaintop will be with us in the storm as a reminder that He is with you, for you, and full of compassion towards what you are walking through.

Jesus is willing to walk right in the middle of the storm you are facing. He's not intimidated by the crashing waves around you.

What are the crashing waves trying to accomplish?

They are battling for your worship.

The crashing waves are trying to get you to give all of your attention to anything other than Jesus. When you aren't focused on Jesus, they begin to distract you from being able to be used in the middle of your circumstances.

When our focus is placed on anything other than Jesus, we tend to think we don't have enough to make a difference in someone's life.

We start to panic. We start to burn out. We start to take our frustrations out on our spouse and kids. We start to think that God has forgotten us. We start operating in our own strength.

When you keep your heart focused on Jesus and you choose to worship soaking wet in the middle of that storm, you can look down at those scraps from past miracles and say like I have said time and time again in my life, "When I was all alone and wanting to take my own life as a young teenager, that same God who was with me then, is with me now. That same God that rescued a teenager partying, doing drugs, and living for himself is the same God who is with me today. That same God who saved a critical, bitter, sarcastic, young man and gave him a purpose in the middle of a baseball field is the same God who is with me now.

That same God who gave me the strength to lead families through abortions, murders, and suicides is the same God who won't leave me today. That same God who saved my first born and healed her from brain surgery when the doctors said it looked impossible is the same God who is with me now. That same God who led Joseph, David, and Daniel to fulfill their purpose in their generation is the same God who will fulfill His purpose in my life.

You need to carry those scraps with you from season to season because they are the fuel that will allow you to continue to serve a cause bigger than yourself. Just like that young boy was a difference-maker, you can be too if you are willing to use what you have been given.

When we set out to plant VIVE, our prayer was to build a church worthy of the calling of the Name we carry in our generation.

Jesus said, "I will build My Church and this world cannot not stop it!"

WHAT WILL YOU BE KNOWN FOR?

Every one of us will be known for something.

When your moment on this planet is over, and family members and friends are looking back at pictures from the past and your face comes up, what will come to their mind? What legacy will you leave your kids and the generation you are part of? If there's anything I'd love for people to hear as long as I have breath in my lungs is this: build your life on Jesus!

Live your life worthy of the calling of the Name you carry. He is enough for your marriage. He is enough for your kids. He is enough for your miracle you are waiting on. Student, He is enough for you to be a difference-maker on your school campus. Don't let anyone label you or define you. You are marked by majesty and chosen to serve this generation and lead people to Jesus. Don't let anyone make you feel insecure or less than, because the great I Am is inside of you. You can live with confidence as a teenager and be a difference maker.

I want to encourage you that Jesus is enough for that addiction you are battling. He is enough for that shame you've been carrying for so many years. Never forget those scraps that He tells us to carry because it's those scraps that will remind you when life gets hard that you are not alone and you are not forgotten.

What an amazing honor to serve our city and show them that there's no one like our God, there is no gift like Jesus and there's no hope like the Gospel.

There is a plan for your life. Don't waste it living for the pleasures of this world. Decide now that you and your family will be all in and let's be faith-filled people believing that the same God who called us is the same God who is going to cover us.

VIVE Culture is a church for the whosoevers. Whatever that looks like, we are just going to pour our lives into reaching as many as we can. Who knows? The next homeless person or executive who is destroying his family by being a workaholic might get saved, be restored to his family, and become one of our staff members at VIVE Culture.

It can happen.

It's not crazy. It's Jesus.

Sometimes people just need to be reminded that they have something worth fighting for. God can restore what the enemy tried to destroy if you have the fight in you to keep going. We all go through tough seasons in life. Maybe you are in one right now. But I want to encourage you: don't quit. Don't quit on your calling. Don't quit on your marriage. Don't give up on your kids. Just because a season is over in your life doesn't mean your story it through.

So many people settle for Costco samples of what God has for them. Why settle for samples when you've been given a seat at the King's table? Don't settle for crumbs. Get up and take another step forward. We have a heart to serve all people. If someone is in front of us, we want to serve them. Our competition isn't other churches that preach Jesus. Our competition is the enemy of our souls who is trying to destroy anything that matters to the heart of God—which is ultimately you and me.

Louie Giglio, lead pastor of Passion City Church, is a hero of mine. He's mentored me from a distance for over two decades. If there's one person I could be personally mentored by and do life with in ministry it would be with Louie—and his Passion Team. The heartbeat and DNA of the Passion movement has infected my wife and me in the best ways. And when Louie stepped out to lead Passion City Church several years ago, before they even had one launch meeting, he said this:

> When we met as a core team, we knew we couldn't afford to wait until we were a mature church, or had a building or a marketing strategy to be outward to the unreached and under-researched of the world. For the very maturing process of becoming all God has intended us to be is in the going.

The enemy isn't playing games and neither are we. Every day our desire is to make heaven more crowded. Hell gets nervous when faith rises up inside of the hearts of God's people and we begin to take back what the enemy tried to steal from us. This is our moment. Our generation. We will not waste our lives, but we intend to make every moment count living for a cause greater than our own.

9

sent to our city

I hope by now you are getting a glimpse of what God wants to do in you and your family to serve the people this generation. By the time you close this book, I want you to get a fresh vision for your life through the lens of Jesus. I want you to get a fresh vision for your marriage, family, and home. Student, I want you to get a fresh vision for what God wants to do on your campus. If you are retired, I want you to get a fresh vision for your life other than just joining the country club and vegging out by the pool. If you have breath in your lungs still, God isn't done using you.

There is a high cost when we don't live with a God-sized vision for our lives.

Where there is no vision, the people cast off restraint.

(Proverbs 29:18 NKJV)

When you don't have a vision from God you live anyway you want. You sleep with whomever you want, spend money however you want, and treat people anyway you want. When you don't have a vision you waste your life living for the pleasures of this world. However, when you receive a mandate from heaven and get a vision for how God wants to use you,

you live with a sense of purpose and identity. Consider what Habakkuk wrote:

> Write the vision and make it plain on tablets, that he may run who reads it. For the vision is yet for an appointed time; but at the end it will speak, and it will not lie. Though it tarries, wait for it; because it will surely come, it will not tarry.

> (Habakkuk 2:2 NKJV)

When vision comes to your life, get ready. I want you to lean in right now on these final pages because I believe God is going to either start or reignite something in your spirit before the end of this book.

God may give you a vision for your life that may not happen for a few years. Young person, God may give you a vision that won't come to pass for a decade. Don't lose hope. VIVE Culture was a fifteen-year vision in the making.

No matter what season of life you are in, know this: you are being sent!

> Then, the same day at evening, being the first day of the week, when the doors were shut where the disciples were assembled, for fear of the Jews, Jesus came and stood in the midst, and said to them, "Peace be with you." When He had said this, He showed them His hands and His side. Then the disciples were glad when they saw the Lord. So Jesus said to them again, "Peace to you! As the Father has sent Me, I also send you."

> (John 20:19–21 NKJV)

Let me give you some quick context to what is happening here. Jesus was sent by God down to earth to rescue and restore humanity to His heart. Jesus came to serve. Jesus did this for the Father's glory. Jesus faithfully served and fulfilled His assignment by giving up His life to be crucified on the cross for the sins of the world.

Jesus was dead three days in the grave, and once and for all, defeated death, hell, and the grave for every sin that humanity would ever commit. You can't sing loud enough, or do enough good deeds to be right with God. Jesus absorbed our rebellion and shame. It wasn't a partnership. It was all Jesus. On the third day Jesus came back to life and the first person He revealed Himself to—to be his mouthpiece—was a woman.

You want to see VIVE Culture get fired up? Have someone tell us that women don't have a place at the leadership table. We will be all over them because in our House my wife and I are co-lead pastors and women have just as strong of a voice as the men, because there is so much power when a passionate, godly woman preaches and leads like Jesus. In our House women are released to lead, preach, and carry great leadership weight that is incredibly valuable to our church.

Jesus revealed Himself and found the disciples hiding out of fear for their lives. Jesus revealed Himself to them, prepared them to be sent out on mission, and them: "As the Father sent Me, now I send you."

You don't need to be a theologian to understand what Jesus is saying.

Our mission is to be sent to be the hands and feet of Jesus.

We are sent by God to occupy our city and neighborhoods with the hope of Jesus.

This isn't a pastor thing.

The call is for wherever you are, live, or work—that is your mission field.

Therefore, go and make disciples of all nations, baptizing them in the name of the Father and of the Son and of the Holy Spirit, and teaching them to obey everything I have commanded you. And surely I am with you always, to the very end of the age.

(Matthew 28:19–20)

The moment you surrender your life to Jesus, you are called to go! The vision you have for your life impacts how you live.

Alicia and I are similar in a lot of ways and love the same types of things. However, by now you know there are a few areas that we are very different. For example, we have vastly different ideas of what our birthdays should look like. The vision I have for a great birthday is to take it easy, smoke some meat, spend time with people I love, and watch sports. Honestly, I don't even care if I get a present.

Alicia, however, grew up with nine other brothers and sisters. So birthdays were a big deal to them. When I got married, I had no idea how big of a deal they were. I've learned over the years that if I want to make her day special, I need to a get a vision for what the day is going to look like.

Last year, I felt inspired to make this the best birthday that my wife would ever have. I wanted to get her something really special. She deserves it. She birthed six humans from her body, homeschools our children, makes home-cooked meals, and still has time to make our house a loving, comfortable home. So I was trying to find the perfect gift.

Nothing was worthy of what she deserved.

It was a few days away from her birthday and I was starting to stress out. I had this vision in my head and my wife wasn't giving me any hints. One Friday night we were sitting on the couch watching TV and this commercial came on.

My wife said, "That that's the thing I was telling you about."

Men, what is that called?

A hint.

I was all over that clue. I got so excited because I was going to get her something that she could actually use. I couldn't mess this one up. I jumped online, bought it, and had it sent to my office so she wouldn't see it ahead of time. I put it in a gift bag and had it waiting for her at the dinner table.

The way we do gifts in my home is we eat dinner as a family first and then we open up presents before we have cake. Honestly, I was eating dinner that night with a little more confidence than I normally do. I knew I'd hit a home run.

I smiled as I thought to myself, "Girl, you have no idea what's coming."

I envisioned her screaming, with a tear slowly falling down her cheek, stunned that I picked up the hint. I couldn't wait for her to finish eating. The moment finally came for her to open up her gift. She grabbed that gift bag and I leaned in, waiting for her reaction. She pulled out the gift and was silent. She gasped and then busted out laughing.

Why was she laughing?

Did she love it? Was it everything she ever wanted? Was she overwhelmed with emotion and trying to find the right words to say?

Holding her present, her eyes got big and with a smile she said, "Wow, a professional water flosser for my mouth."

I got her a water flosser!

Why?

Why would I ever think that a woman would love a water flosser for her birthday?

Alicia started cracking up wondering what in the world I was thinking. It turns out the reason she wasn't giving me any hints for the weeks leading up to her birthday was because she knew if she said anything I would run out and buy it. And women are cruel. Instead of returning it and getting something she loved, she set that water flosser on the bathroom sink for two weeks—still in its packaging—just to remind me of my failure as a husband. Every time my wife and two oldest daughters would walk by the sink, they would start laughing.

I thought it was a very thoughtful and practical gift.

It's not about simply getting a vision for your life.

It's about getting the right vision for your life.

JESUS IS IN THE SENDING BUSINESS

It is so much easier to live out the vision God has for you when you are planted around others who share the same values and passions. If you want to lose weight, it is so much easier when you have a workout partner. If you want a great marriage, plant yourself around other people who have a great marriage. If you want to be a great parent, stay around other parents who share the same values. If you want to make an impact in people's lives with the finances you've been given, surround yourself with other generous people.

The vision you have for your life impacts the way you live.

Jesus said, "As the Father sent Me so I also send you."

Jesus is in the sending business. God's primary concern isn't your time-share and retirement plan. His primary concern isn't in families playing it safe and holding on until Jesus comes back. He is interested in reaching people far from Him. Throughout the Bible, God sent people to get out of their comfort zones, leave the known, and impact cities so people could be reconnected to the Father's heart.

God sent Abram to a land and he didn't even know what was waiting for him when he got there. God said, "Go, and I'll reveal the plan over time." He sent Moses to speak to Pharaoh and Moses didn't know how that would work out. He was simply sent by God and had to work through the process as he went. God sent John the Baptist to prepare the way of the Lord. God sent Elisha, David, Samuel, Paul, and Peter—and he is sending you and your family as well.

Growing up I would always hear Christians say, "We can't wait to bring people to church so they can meet Jesus."

As I have grown in my relationship with Jesus I realize now that sounds cute but that isn't actually the call of Jesus followers. The call is for us to bring Jesus to people. At VIVE Culture we aren't waiting for people to come to our church. Our passion is to take Jesus to the streets. That means when we go to the city, we are taking Jesus to people. When we go to the suburbs, we are taking Jesus to people. When we are on the soccer fields, we are taking Jesus to people. When we are at the pool, we are taking Jesus to people. When we go to Hollywood, you got it, we are taking Jesus to people.

Jesus didn't wait for us to come to Him. Jesus came to us before we even decided to follow Him.

God sent Jesus. Jesus is now sending us to every corner of the planet with the hope of the gospel.

Jesus is in the sending business. When we get that truth in our spirits it changes how we live our lives.

That means we can lead with love no matter how people vote, what lifestyle people have chosen, or what god they have chosen to worship. Jesus is passionate about reaching every single human on the planet.

I'm so thankful we don't have to go out on our own because we are being sent by God.

VIVE Culture isn't a pastor thing. Our church is a Jesus thing. I love what Brian Houston once said: "The Church isn't built on the talented few, but by the sacrifices of many people."

If you are a follower of Jesus, you are being sent. Jesus loves to send people to represent His kingdom. You have been sent to your job, your campus, and your neighborhood. It's not an accident that you have the friends you have.

I hear people tell me, "My faith is just private."

There is no such thing as a private faith.

There is no such thing as a private Christian. You can have a private devotional life. You can have private prayer time. But there is no such thing as a private Christian. In any other area of life, we would say that is ridiculous. Just think about it.

I'm a die-hard Chicago Bears fan. We hate the Green Bay Packers. It's one of the greatest and longest rivals in all of sports. No one shows up to the game undecided. No one is trying to blend in. That's ridiculous. Everyone wears their shirts, paints their faces, and is ready to let the world know whom they are cheering for.

Humans are wired to go public with the things they care most about.

You may be the only person that can reach your coworker who is on the verge of divorce. You may be the only person who can reach that student who is thinking about taking his or her own life. Jesus is in the sending business to reach our city.

God has a specific plan on where He sends His people. Our job is to be faithful to the vision. His job is to be faithful to the promise.

God is willing to do whatever it takes for us to reach people far from Him. He is willing to send us wherever is needed to build families. And it all starts with receiving a fresh vision for your life.

Isaiah 6 describes a man who received a vision for his life. And every time a person receives a vision, the point of that vision is to go and do something about it:

In the year that King Uzziah died, I saw the Lord sitting on a throne, high and lifted up, and the train of His robe filled the temple. Above it stood seraphim; each one had six wings: with two he covered his face, with two he covered his feet, and with two he flew. And one cried to another and said: "Holy, holy, holy is the LORD of hosts; the whole earth is full of His glory!" And the posts of the door were shaken by the voice of him who cried out, and the house was filled with smoke. So I said: "Woe is me, for I am undone!

Because I am a man of unclean lips, and I dwell in the midst of a people of unclean lips; For my eyes have seen the King, the Lord of hosts."

(Isaiah 6:1–5 NKJV)

One of our anchor points at VIVE is worship. It's not something we do; it's who we are. There is something about music that moves the human heart that is hard to describe. We were created to be worshipers. We create worship experiences through VIVE Culture Music that are passionate, powerful, and moving because we know that when people encounter Jesus, people begin to get a vision of who He is and what He has in store for them.

When people encounter Jesus, the most normal thing imaginable isn't to sit there and do nothing. When people's lives collide with His there is always a response.

Sometimes the response is raising our hands, or shouting, kneeling, crying, singing, or dancing. When you have a real encounter with Jesus, you realize that you would be dead if it weren't for His grace. Isaiah saw this vision and how worship was changing the atmosphere where he was standing. People weren't standing around watching his vision. Everyone was fully engaged as participants.

Then one of the seraphim flew to me, having in his hand a live coal which he had taken with the tongs from the altar. And he touched my mouth with it, and said: "Behold, this has touched your lips; Your iniquity is taken away, and your sin purged."

(Isaiah 6:6–7 NKJV)

What a powerful picture of the gospel. That's grace. Notice Isaiah didn't do anything to earn that. We had a debt that we could not pay and Jesus paid a debt He did not owe so you could walk in freedom today. That's how good God is. While we were still sinners, He was sent to rescue and restore us back to God's heart. We can't earn it. We don't deserve it. Because of His grace, we are completely forgiven.

I can't get enough of the grace of Jesus.

But look what Isaiah describes next:

Also I heard the voice of the Lord, saying: "Whom shall I send, and who will go for Us?"

(Isaiah 6:8a NKJV)

Basically the Lord was saying, "I want everyone in the world to experience this grace. I want everyone to know this freedom. Who will be willing to get out of their comfort zone and go? Who is willing to use their influence, their gift of making money, or their gifts to attract people to lead people to my heart? Who is willing to do what it takes for a lost and dying world to know this type of grace."

When you have that type of vision and experience that type of forgiveness of course the only appropriate response is what Isaiah said:

Here am I! Send me.

(Isaiah 6:8b NKJV)

This isn't the person who says, "I just grew up in church my whole life and this is all I know." This is the type of person who understands who they were apart from Jesus.

And now that they are saved and called to be part of the greatest story in all of history, their response is, "Pick me!"

Use my money.
Use my gifts.
Use my voice.
Use my house.
Use my time.
It's all Yours, anyway.
Send me.

JESUS ISN'T STUCK WITH YOU . . .
HE CHOSE YOU

When I was growing up, I played sports all year long. One of my favorite sports was basketball. It still is. As a kid, we'd head to the playground and play hoops for hours with our friends. And every playground had that one kid whose skills didn't match up with their love for the game. We all know that one kid that I'm talking about.

Maybe you were that one kid. It's okay. We all have something we are good at.

I always felt bad for that one kid because he would show up early to warm up, have his headband on, his socks pulled all the way up to his knees, and be ready to go.

There was always that one kids whose swag never matched up with his game on the court. They looked good but they just didn't have the skill set to ball.

When it came time to pick teams, there were always two captains. Each captain would have a chance to pick one player at a time until there was no one left.

I hated that ranking system—not because I was ever picked last, but because I knew that one kid would always be picked last.

The first captain would say, "I got him."

The second captain would say, "I pick him."

And they'd go all the way down until the last poor kid was left.

I never wanted to make eye contact with that player. I would always pretend to stretch or bend down to tie my shoes, even though they were already tied. It came to that awkward moment when the second captain would finally say, "And I pick him."

Everyone on the playground knew the second captain didn't pick that player; they were stuck with him. That is not much of a confidence booster when you feel like your team is stuck with you. When you are *that* player, you run around the court while no one passes you the ball.

Here's the good news God doesn't have a ranking system like that. He isn't looking throughout the earth looking for the most gifted and talented. He isn't looking for who has the most social media followers.

For the eyes of the Lord throughout the earth to strengthen those whose hearts are fully committed to him.

(2 Chronicles 16:9a)

God's ranking system is much different than how we used to do it playing ball on the blacktop. God doesn't feel like He's stuck with you or me. In fact, He's been pursuing you since the day you were born. He shaped you and planted you in your city for such a time as this. He is inviting you to be part of what He is doing in this generation.

Isaiah got this vision in his heart and he saw that God was up to something big that He was about to unleash on earth—and Isaiah raised his hand and said, "Send me." Isaiah didn't know where, he didn't know how, and he didn't how much it was going to cost. There was no marketing strategy and no launch team. He didn't know if he'd lose all his friends or who would try to talk him out of it.

All Isaiah knew was that He received a vision and knew God was up to something, and he said, "Here I am. Send me."

There are so many people who are waiting for someone to be sent their way to get a fresh vision for their lives. In whatever season you are in, if we will choose to be worshipers, and keep our focus on Jesus, Jesus can use us to reach the whosoevers.

About midnight Paul and Silas were praying and singing hymns to God, and the other prisoners were listening to them.

(Acts 16:25)

Something powerful happens when a person chooses to worship in the middle of whatever circumstances they are walking through. People take notice. Don't miss how, once again, worship was the theme here.

Suddenly there was such a violent earthquake that the foundations of the prison were shaken. At once all the prison doors flew open, and everyone's chains came loose. The jailer woke up, and when he saw the prison doors open, he drew his sword and was about to kill himself because he thought the prisoners had escaped.

(Acts 16:26–27)

Let me give some context to this story. Paul and Silas were beaten and thrown into prison—for a mission that Jesus had sent them on. You would have thought that Jesus got this mission wrong. If Jesus sent them, how in the world did they end up in prison?

It's easy for us to complain about bad days or tough seasons. "Jesus, it's all Your fault I'm where I am," we say.

In reality, Paul and Silas were sent to that cold, dark prison cell because there was a family that God needed to reach. Lost people matter to God and they should matter to us. Every single story matters to the heart of God.

Paul and Silas could have played the "poor me" card.

But Paul and Silas were men with a vision for their life.

Those prisoners were listening to Paul and Silas. And in the middle of the night, there was something so powerful happening in that worship service that all the prison doors flew open and the prisoners' chains were released. There is something powerful that happens during worship when God begins to move and our chains and bondages that entrap us are broken in Jesus' Name.

Now can I be honest with you? If it were me, and the doors flew open and my chains broke loose, I would see that as a sign from heaven that it was God's will to run for the hills. I'm just being honest. You would have thought that, too, if you didn't have a vision for your life. Paul and Silas knew they weren't abandoned. They were sent.

> But Paul shouted, "Don't harm yourself! We are all here!" The jailer called for lights, rushed in and fell trembling before Paul and Silas. He then brought them out and asked, "Sirs, what must I do to be saved?" They replied, "Believe in the Lord Jesus, and you will be saved—you and your household." Then they spoke the word of the LORD to him and to all the others in his house. At that hour of the night the jailer took them and washed their wounds; then immediately he and all his household were baptized. The jailer brought them into his house and set a meal before them; he was filled with joy because he had come to believe in God—he and his whole household.
>
> (Acts 16:28–34)

Who was baptized? His entire household. Men, don't ever underestimate the power of leading your family spiritually. I have such a passion to see men come to faith and grasp a vision for their life, because when that happens, their entire home will be impacted.

VIVE Culture strives to build a family church because we believe there is something powerful that can happen in our city when an entire family comes to know Jesus. When kids grasp a vision for what God has for their life, it's powerful. Our kid's ministries aren't babysitting services. Our goal isn't to teach kids how to be "good kids." We want them to be *godly* kids who grow up to be mission-driven adults. We want our kids to be taught what it means to be passionate worshipers, and we want them to learn the Bible.

We want the kids and students that come out of VIVE to have mindset that wherever they are, they are being sent by God.

There's something magnificent that happens when the people of God get a vision from heaven.

LOOK FOR WAYS TO BE A BLESSING

Let me just take the pressure off of you. There already was a hero and His Name is Jesus! Our role is to lead people to Jesus and be a blessing everywhere we go.

So many people think if they don't have a vision to speak to 100,000 people, then their vision isn't a God-sized vision. Really? Most of the life-change stories Jesus was involved with didn't occur when He was preaching.

Do you realize that?

Almost every story where people encounter Jesus is when He was doing life with people. In my mind, Jesus was funny, loved to have fun with his team, and loved to share life with other people.

Jesus was one of those leaders who looked for opportunities to be a blessing. Jesus took time to notice people.

> Jesus entered Jericho and was passing through. A man was there by the name of Zacchaeus; he was a chief tax collector and was wealthy. He wanted to see who Jesus was, but because he was short he could not see over the crowd.

> (Luke 19:1–3)

Jesus was "passing through" Jericho. In other words, He wasn't there for a scheduled appointment. Once again, we see a tax collector—considered to be one of the worst of sinners— intrigued by Jesus. Zacchaeus, who didn't yet have a relationship with Jesus, tried to do whatever it took to find out what was so attractional about this man.

So he ran ahead and climbed a sycamore-fig tree to see him, since Jesus was coming that way. When Jesus reached the spot, he looked up and said to him, "Zacchaeus, come down immediately. I must stay at your house today." So he came down at once and welcomed him gladly. All the people saw this and began to mutter, "He has gone to be the guest of a sinner."

(Luke 19:4–7)

This is both humorous and tragic. The religious people set up a ranking system of who was "good" enough to share life with them. Religious people would never dare to share life with anyone who didn't believe, vote, or parent like them. Jesus looked up and saw Zacchaeus in that tree and Jesus locked eyes with Zacchaeus for the first time.

Who knows what Zacchaeus was thinking. Likely he was thinking that there was no way Jesus would want to speak with him—he was a tax collector! No one wanted to spend time with tax collectors. But men like Zacchaeus were the reason Jesus was sent to earth.

I picture Jesus looking up and having the biggest smile on His face. There Zacchaeus was. Jesus' countenance wasn't full of disappointment. Knowing Jesus, His face was beaming with pride. To Jesus, Zacchaeus wasn't a tax collector. He was a child of God. Jesus made time to spend with him. Zacchaeus wasn't interrupting Jesus' mission.

Zacchaeus was the mission.

But Zacchaeus stood up and said to the Lord, "Look, Lord! Here and now I give half of my possessions to the poor, and if I have cheated anybody out of anything, I will pay back four times the amount." Jesus said to him, "Today salvation has come to this house, because this man, too, is a son of Abraham. For the Son of Man came to seek and to save the lost."

(Luke 19:8–10)

What changed? More rules? More Bible memorization? Long church services?

What changed Zacchaeus' heart was a relationship.

When people know you care, they are far more likely to listen to what you have to say than when they feel like a project. Jesus' missional focus was never to go and plant churches. It was never to go and build bigger buildings. Those things are needed, but the missional focus of Jesus was to go and make disciples.

Changed people, change people.

It's about relationships.

The Church isn't an organization you join, it's a family you belong to.

It's about relationships.

Knowing Jesus, He would have gone to Zacchaeus' house even if he didn't have a heart change. That's who Jesus is. Jesus allowed people to follow even before they believed. It's a process.

Notice Jesus' words: Zacchaeus was a son of Abraham.

That means he had the same right to be a child of God as those religious people. Jesus wasn't sent to reach a people group with a certain skin color or a group of people that made a certain amount of money. He came to break all categories and show us that He is about reaching all people groups.

If you want to know God's will for your life today, you can choose to wake up every day and say, "Wherever I am, I am going to be the biggest blessing."

You be the biggest blessing when you show up to work every day.
You be the biggest blessing when you sow and serve the church you are planted in.
You be the biggest blessing to your spouse and kids.
You be the biggest blessing to your leaders that you are under.
You be the biggest blessing to the coffee shop server when they are taking your order.
You be the biggest blessing when you are ordering food at a restaurant.

You will be amazed how you can serve someone just by choosing to be a blessing everywhere you go.

Even though I am free of the demands and expectations of everyone, I have voluntarily become a servant to any and all in order to reach a wide range of people: religious, nonreligious, meticulous moralists, loose-living immoralists, the defeated, the demoralized—whoever. I didn't take on their way of life. I kept my bearings in Christ—but I entered their world and tried to experience things from their point of view. I've become just about every sort of servant there is in my attempts to lead those I meet into a God-saved life. I did all this because of the Message. I didn't just want to talk about it; I wanted to be in on it!

(1 Corinthians 9:19–23 MSG)

The time for Christians talking about serving is over. Those days are behind us.

We want in on it.

By the time you close this book, my hope is that you will stand with the apostle Paul and say, "I want in on it."

I don't just want to talk about it. I want in on it. I want to build something that will outlast my time here on earth.

What God cares about building more than anything else is people. The only way to build people is to serve them. You can't serve people you don't love.

Let me pose a question: Does what you're building in your life match what God is building? It's an important question to ask. Jesus is about building people. Jesus was just passing through, and because of that divine appointment, an entire household was changed. Jesus said Zacchaeus was a son of Abraham.

That is mind-blowing to think about. Everyone else labeled him a sinner, outcast, and waste of time. Zacchaeus, to the religious people, was one of "those" people. I'm so thankful Jesus came to earth to serve "those" people because there was a time in all of our lives that we were part of that category. Jesus wasn't so preoccupied with getting to the cross that He couldn't make time for people.

The journey is where the joy is. So get a vision for your city and ask God to open your eyes to the needs around you. Don't be so destination focused that you miss out on the journey. Some people are so preoccupied with where they are going that they miss the opportunity to impact a life. Enjoy the journey and bring your family along for the ride. One of the best things we can do for our kids is to let them see Jesus working in and through us by serving people.

OUR CITY IS OUR HOME

I love being at home with my family. I'm a homebody by nature. I recently read an article, though, that stunned me. It said that this generation doesn't necessary travel more than other generations but it *dreams* of traveling more than any other generation. Companies put teasers out for their employees to work hard to make them millions of dollars not to send them on their dream vacation, but rather to get them to dream of it. They sell images. Sometimes being in another place seems much more enjoyable than being home.

Most people don't dream about being anywhere else besides home. We look at the rich and famous and want that life. But home? Nothing great happens at home.

I wonder if that mentality undermines the mission God has for our lives. It's so easy for us to want to serve other nations but ignore the person in need on our own street.

Jesus took great care of and was concerned for his hometown. Global travel to impact the nations is rising. Everyone wants to go here and there, which is incredible. We need to be part of the mission's movement to reach the nations. In saying that, I'm praying for more churches with a heart for their own city first, churches that have planted people who interact with human needs right where their people live.

For us, our primary mission field is the city we live in. There will be times to travel here and there and plant churches. But when people look back at where VIVE is now (and where this church will be in the future), history will attest to the fact that this was where God called this church. These are our family members, friends, and coworkers. History will record not so much what we did in foreign lands—although that's important—but what we did as a local community faithfully in the mission field God planted us in.

We are not called to be the Savior. Thank God for that. All we can do is serve our guts out and share the Good News about Jesus. Our call is to love all and serve all. It's the gospel that brands the hearts of people. The gospel has been etched in our soul and we can't shake it. We see movements throughout history start through ordinary people interacting with other ordinary people.

Sow the gospel in your city—and the only way to sow the gospel is by serving your city. It's not so much in what you say, but how you live every day of your life. I'm convinced that everyday experiences open doors for people to be awakened to the love of Jesus. Ask questions and share life with people who are different than you. Don't lead with blanket statements, but be open to conversations. Learn to be vulnerable and walk with people even if they don't believe what you believe. Let Jesus do the work. Believe in people. That's a great way to start serving them.

I don't let anyone put expectations on me that aren't backed up by what Jesus expects of me. I'm going to make friends and I'm going to walk with people who think and believe different than me. I'm going to speak life into people today, and into their future, believing God will come through. I'm going to hold on, and if I don't receive the full promise in my lifetime, I'm going to pass the baton of faith on to Kaitlyn, Makayla, Riley, Brooklyn, London, Jude, and the next generation.

Sermons can't produce this type of passion to occupy all streets in our city.
Programs can't do it.
Great music can't do it.
Cool slogans or trendy videos can't produce this type of passion.
We have one life and one chance to impact people.

CAUSE OVER COMFORT

When the people heard this, they were cut to the heart and said to Peter and the other apostles, "Brothers, what shall we do?" Peter replied, "Repent and be baptized, every one of you, in the name of Jesus Christ for the forgiveness of your sins. The promise is for you and your children and for all who are far off—for all whom the LORD our God will call." Those who accepted his message were baptized, and about three thousand were added to their number that day. They devoted themselves to the apostles' teaching and to fellowship, to the breaking of bread and to prayer.

Everyone was filled with awe at the many wonders and signs performed by the apostles. All the believers were together and had everything in common. They sold property and possessions to give to anyone who had need. Every day they continued to meet together in the temple courts. They broke bread in their homes and ate together with glad and sincere hearts, praising God and enjoying the favor of all the people. And the LORD added to their number daily those who were being saved.

(Acts 2:37–47)

Numbers do matter. Every number has a name, every name has a story, and every story matters to the heart of God.

The movement in Acts didn't happen because of the talented few. The New Testament Church exploded because the people were so passionate, so loving, so ridiculously generous with their finances, and so unbelievably generous with their words that people couldn't help but want what was in them.

They held tight to the vision for their generation and served that vision with everything they had.

I don't know about you, but I don't want to just read about movements like this. I want to experience it for myself.

I want my kids to see and personally experience God's goodness so it impacts their kids, and their kids' kids after them.

My prayer is that, as we come to the end of this book, you aren't discontent with where you are at but feel inspired to bloom where you are planted.

Perhaps your marriage isn't where you want it to be yet—keep fighting for it. Maybe your kids aren't where you want them to be in their spiritual journey, but keep speaking life into them. Stay committed to loving them through the process. You may not have the dream job you want yet, but keep asking God to open your eyes for opportunities to be used to serve your coworkers. You don't have to keep peeking over the fence at everyone's social media feeds and feeling like you are missing out. Get a vision for the city you live in and do everything you can to plant in a local church and ensure that your family flourishes there.

When we get to heaven, we won't regret one moment of intersecting with our community to meet human needs so that as many as would receive Him would come to know the power and faithfulness of our God. Oftentimes, the biggest movements where people come to know Jesus are when people are simply doing life with other people.

This generation more than any other has a real desire for transparency, authenticity, and honesty. People identify much more with our failures than they do our successes. Don't be afraid to open up to people.

The goal isn't to simply serve people to meet their physical needs. Yes, that is part of it and we have a vision for that. What people need more than anything is Jesus. It's a regeneration of the heart.

When it comes to the gospel, we've got to be as real as we possibly can or we end up becoming white noise and finding our place among all the other shining lights and flashing memos that people are bombarded with. Even people who don't believe in Jesus are finding ways to meet human needs. That's part of being part of the human race.

What makes Jesus followers different? The gospel.

At the end of the day the gospel is what is needed in our generation more than anything else.

We need people of faith who will occupy all streets with the Good News. We need people of faith who can walk through difficult storms and still passionately worship and say, "God, You're so good!"

We're faith people.

This transcends positivity or optimism and is anchored in the Word of God and His promises. He's a good God. One day you will stand in the presence of God when you get to heaven and it won't matter what kind of timeshare you owned or how much money you had in the bank. One day, someone else will be sitting in your seat, with your title on the door.

Fifty years from now most people won't even remember your name. Husband, that company you are giving your family up for may not even be around in twenty years. Mom, you only get one chance to have this time with your kids. Student, you only have one time in life to impact other students God has placed around you. Grandparents, you only get one season to invest in your grandchildren and speak life into them and show them what a godly, passionate follower of Jesus really looks like.

Once it's gone…it's gone!

Don't waste your life.

Therefore, it is of faith that it might be according to grace, so that the promise might be sure to all the seed, not only to those who are of the law, but also to those who are of the faith of Abraham, who is the father of us all (as it is written, "I have made you a father of many nations") in the presence of Him whom he believed—God, who gives life to the dead and calls those things which do not exist as though they did.

(Romans 4:16–17 NKJV)

Only Jesus can bring dead things back to life again! Only Jesus can restore a broken marriage, heal a wounded heart, or allow a heart to be born again.

I would love to leave you with this encouragement:

Say to them, "The Lord bless you and keep you; The Lord make His face shine upon you, and be gracious to you; The Lord lift up His countenance upon you, and give you peace."

(Numbers 6:23–26 ESV)

The light of the gospel is distorted by the inconsistency of the faces of God's people in this generation. Your face oftentimes trumpets your words. You have no idea what a difference a smile can make in a person's life. Sometimes you need to remind your face that you are saved. You need to tell your face you are happy. I want the last thing you think of when you close this book is how God is looking at you right now.

You may be in a broken marriage and are doing everything you can to hold on to hope. You may have been running from God and feel like He's ashamed of you. You may be wrestling through anger because someone horrifically robbed you of your innocence. You may be someone who has been coasting by, working endlessly for a paycheck, and missing out on God's vision for your life.

Wherever you are in life please know this:

You are valued.
You are approved.
You are chosen.
You are called.
You are loved.
You are prized.
Jesus smiles with approval for you.
He's proud of you.

You can't do anything to make Jesus love you any more or any less than He does at this very moment.

For God, who said, "Let there be light in the darkness," has made this light shine in our hearts so we could know the glory of God that is seen in the face of Jesus Christ.

(2 Corinthians 4:6 NLT)

How would you lead your home, spend your money, raise your kids, run your business, or lead your employees if you knew God Himself was always smiling with approval? How would you interact with your city if you really understood how deeply He loves you and wants to have a relationship with everyone you meet?

When you get a vision of how God looks at you and me, it changes how we love and serve people.

Vision is a picture of the future that creates passion in people.

We are not in it for ourselves to make the headlines on social media. We are in it for future generations because we are just another page in the grand story of God that is unfolding before us. And when our time is done on this earth and our chapter in history is over, we want to look back and say we built something that will outlast us that will be felt for generations.

I love what Bill Hybels, former pastor of Willow Creek Church for over thirty-five years, said:

> There's nothing in the world like the local church when the local church is working right. Lost people are getting found, and found people are growing up, and lonely people are getting enfolded, and bored people are finding a purpose and a cause, and the poor are being cared for. Because I believe the local church is the hope of the world. And if we are too busy to pack seats with people who need hope, we're too busy.

To that I say, Amen!

Dietrich Bonhoeffer, a German Lutheran pastor and participant in the German resistance movement against Nazism, saw that the local church was more than just gathering people on the weekends. It was about serving those in need. In fact, he was involved with members of the German Military Intelligence Office's plans to assassinate Adolf Hitler. His involvement led to his arrest in April of 1943, and he was later executed by hanging in April of 1945. He was a pastor and was committed to giving his entire life to take out an evil man who made it his mission to wipe out an entire people group from the face of the earth.

Bonhoeffer couldn't stand by and do nothing.

He broke the mold in his time in history when he said, "The Church is only the Church when it exists for others."

There is a real enemy committed to destroying your life and everyone you love. As a church—knowing what the enemy is committed to—we are committed to giving our lives to provide every person the opportunity to connect to God's heart and grow in their spiritual journey.

We are a visual, story-driven generation and we want to make our lives count!

God has a job to do on this earth. He's about redeeming, restoring, and rebuilding.

He's going to look at you and me and ask one day, "Were you faithful?"

Jesus didn't just come to save you from something. He saved you *for* something as well. And that's a life of service.

So my hope is that you close this book and have a fresh vision to do something. Faithfulness requires action. I pray you will be motivated by what Christ has done for you to join the global Church to build something that will outlast you and me. No, the church isn't perfect. It's messy at times. There are things to work through because it's a family.

Even so, Jesus chose us to build His Church in our generation, and from the bottom of our hearts, we really do love the Church.

What a privilege it is to serve the generation we live in. Let's commit to be people who, together, give our lives to pursue a spirit of servanthood.

Stay planted.

Stay faithful.

Stay full of vision to serve the people around you.

To me, that's living.

That's plain enough, isn't it? You're no longer wandering exiles. This kingdom of faith is now your home country. You're no longer strangers or outsiders. You belong here, with as much right to the name Christian as anyone. God is building a home. He's using us all—irrespective of how we got here—in what He is building. He used the apostles and prophets for the foundation. Now he's using you, fitting you in brick by brick, stone by stone, with Christ Jesus as the cornerstone that holds all the parts together. We see it taking shape day after day—a holy temple built by God—all of us built into it—a temple in which God is quite at home.

(Ephesians 2:19–22 MSG)

THE BEST INVITATION

I don't want to miss an opportunity to give people a chance to respond to the invitation Jesus gives to each person, to give their entire hearts to Him.

I want you to know that no matter what you've done or what's been done to you, you can't make Jesus love you any more or any less than He does at this very moment. What Jesus has done for you is greater than anything anyone could ever do to you. There are consequences to sin but we know that the same answer to every sin that exists is only found in Jesus.

Trust me when I say that choosing to be a follower of Jesus will be the single most important decision you will ever make. That doesn't mean it's a get-out-of-jail free card to pain, heartache, or suffering, or that everything will instantly change the moment you choose to follow Him. But it does ensure that we never have to go through life alone.

In Christ, you have an advocate who is relentlessly in love with you and will never abandon you. Because of the cross, you have direct access to God and the best part isn't the blessings that come through Jesus. The real prize is Jesus Himself. Our future in heaven is forever secure the moment we choose to place our hope in Him.

The decision to make Jesus the Lord and Savior of your heart will have an impact that will outlast you. It will impact your kids, grandkids, and great grandkids. The choice is up to you.

This day I call the heavens and the earth as witnesses against you that I have set before you life and death, blessings and curses. Now choose life, so that you and your children may live.

(Deuteronomy 30:19)

I believe God still has more for your life. I believe God had a specific plan for you when He created you. I believe there's nothing too big or small that you could ever do that Jesus can't forgive and use to help other people.

It's amazing how many people walk through life always thinking God's mad at them. He's not mad at you. He's proud of you. He's in love with you. You were created to be in relationship with Him. He wants you to come back home.

The only way you can be in right standing with God is through His Son, Jesus.

The only way to be a son or daughter of God is through Jesus.

It's not in how long you have been going to church.
It's not in how many songs you can sing.
It's not in how good a person you are.
You can't earn this free gift. It has to be accepted.

The only way to be right with God and have your future in heaven secure is through Jesus. He loves you so much that He wants you to come just as you are. But He loves you way too much to let you stay that way:

If you declare with your mouth, "Jesus is Lord," and believe in your heart that God raised him from the dead, you will be saved. For it is with your heart that you believe and are justified, and it is with your mouth that you profess your faith and are saved. As Scripture says, "Anyone who believes in him will never be put to shame." For there is no difference between Jew and Gentile—the same Lord is Lord of all and richly blesses all who call on him, for, "Everyone who calls on the name of the Lord will be saved."

(Romans 10:9–13)

There are things in life that we can be wrong about and it's not a big deal. But we cannot be wrong about our eternal destination. Heaven and hell are the only two options waiting for every human being and Jesus is the only way to be brought near to God. God sent Jesus so that all people would one day choose to place their hope in Him.

> I write these things to you who believe in the name of the Son of God so that you may know that you have eternal life.

(1 John 5:13)

Be absolutely sure!

I still have a long way to go and have so much to learn. I'm nowhere near where I want to be in my walk with Jesus. The longer I walk with Jesus the more I realize how little I really know. But I will tell you one thing: if Jesus didn't answer one more of my prayers, what He did on the cross over two thousand years ago would have been more than enough for me to give my entire life to Him.

There is nothing in this world that compares to how amazing His love is. I'm so in love with Him. His grace changed everything for me. This has nothing to do with a religion. It's all about a relationship.

Christianity isn't an argument...it's a confession!

Jesus knows every single sin you've ever done, or will do, and still came so you could be completely forgiven. When you accept Jesus, you are not partially forgiven. You are completely forgiven. In Luke 23:43, as Jesus was hanging on the cross in the final moments of His life, one of the criminals hanging on the cross next to him confessed that he was a sinner and believed in Jesus.

How did Jesus respond?

Jesus said, "Today you will be with me in paradise."

Guilt is the starting point for grace.

That criminal never led anyone to Jesus. He never put a dime in the offering bucket. He never attended a church service. He was never baptized. He never served on a mission trip. He did absolutely nothing to earn his salvation. He admitted his guilt and confessed Jesus as Lord—and through Jesus he is in heaven for eternity.

I can just picture Jesus' smile in those final moments looking at that criminal, and it reminds me that this is why He came. He came for you and for me.

It should have been you and me on that cross; Jesus paid for our sin, shame, and rebellion with His life.

You will never be able to be right with God until you admit you are a sinner and in need of a Savior. Jesus didn't come to save heroes. He came to save sinners. He's not interested in trying to make an improved version of you. He wants to make you a new creation.

Therefore, if anyone is in Christ, the new creation has come: The old has gone, the new is here!

(2 Corinthians 5:17)

This free gift I'm talking about has nothing to do with how good you are, but everything to do with how good Jesus is. It is only by His grace that we can be saved.

It's amazing how many people I talk to who feel forgotten and abandoned because of what they have done. I assure you that when God looks at you, He is pleased with you.

"So—who is like me? Who holds a candle to me?" says The Holy. Look at the night skies: Who do you think made all this? Who marches this army of stars out each night, counts them off, calls each by name — so magnificent! so powerful! — and never overlooks a single one?

(Isaiah 40:26 MSG)

If God knows every star by name and leads them out one-by-one, I promise you, He has not forgotten about you. You are not overlooked. You are known and you are loved.

But because of his great love for us, God, who is rich in mercy, made us alive with Christ even when we were dead in transgressions—it is by grace you have been saved. And God raised us up with Christ and seated us with him in the heavenly realms in Christ Jesus, in order that in the coming ages he might show the incomparable riches of his grace, expressed in his kindness to us in Christ Jesus. For it is by grace you have been saved, through faith—and this is not from yourselves, it is the gift of God—not by works, so that no one can boast.

(Ephesians 2:4–9)

He took you and me at our worst, gave us His best, and then wove us into His masterful plan to be part of His story. You are marked by majesty and He's not through with you yet.

If you haven't yet made that decision to be a follower of Jesus, allow me the privilege of walking you through a simple prayer that will be the beginning of a brand-new purpose for your life.

Just repeat after me wherever you find yourself right now:

Dear heavenly Father, I know I am a sinner. I am sorry and choose today to accept Jesus as the Lord and Savior of my life. I believe Jesus died for my sins and that You raised Him to life. I want to trust Him with my life and follow Him from this day forward. Jesus, I put my trust in You and I surrender my life to You. Please come into my life. I pray this in the Name of Jesus. Amen.

If you prayed that prayer, I want you to know that all of heaven is cheering for you. You are not a better version of what you once were, but instead you are a new creation. You are totally forgiven.

Let me encourage you that this isn't the end; this is just the beginning of a brand-new journey. I want to encourage you to find a Christian church in your area this week and begin growing in your faith. We were never intended to do life alone. I believe the hope of the world is the local church.

It is the one thing that Jesus said can never be stopped.

The local church is unstoppable.

So get yourself planted in a healthy, thriving, passionate church that is focused on serving their city and world.

The best thing we can do to serve our world is to tell them about this Good News that changed everything for us!

Jesus is the best thing that has ever happened to us . . . there's not even a close second.

about the author

Brian and Alicia are the founding pastors of VIVE Culture in Kansas City, Missouri. Brian has a very personal, vulnerable way of communicating where he uses humor and real-life stories that bring the Bible to life in ways people can apply to their everyday lives. His passion for life and people is reflected in how he leads. They both have a deep passion to build families in their local church and see people flourish in their gifts.

Prior to planting VIVE Culture, over the last fifteen years Brian was a student's pastor, family pastor, and creative arts pastor. Brian has traveled around the country leading worship, speaking and has recorded a few worship albums.

He has a love for music, smoking meat, and is a die-hard pro sports fan. He continues to pray that one-day God will send Kansas City an NBA and NHL team that will one day become world champions.

Made in the USA
Lexington, KY
07 August 2018